NEWCOMER PHONICS

Teacher's Guide

Kaye Wiley • Gary Apple

LONGMAN

Addison Wesley Longman

New York • London • Hong Kong

Newcomer Phonics
Teacher's Guide

Addison Wesley Longman, 10 Bank Street, White Plains, NY 10606

Executive editor: Anne Stribling
Development editor: Yoko Mia Hirano
Director of design and production: Rhea Banker
Managing editor: Linda Moser
Production manager: Alana Zdinak
Senior production editor: Mike Kemper
Cover design: Rhea Banker
Senior manufacturing manager: Patrice Fraccio
Text design: Elizabeth Carlson
Text composition: TSI Graphics

Assessment and practice pages: Curt Belshe
Illustrations: Kathryn Adams, Megan Montague Cash, Chris Reed, Michael Sloan
Photography: All studio photography by Ken Karp

ISBN: 0-201-38556-2
1 2 3 4 5 6 7 8 9 10–BAH–03 02 01 00 99

Meet the Phonics Team

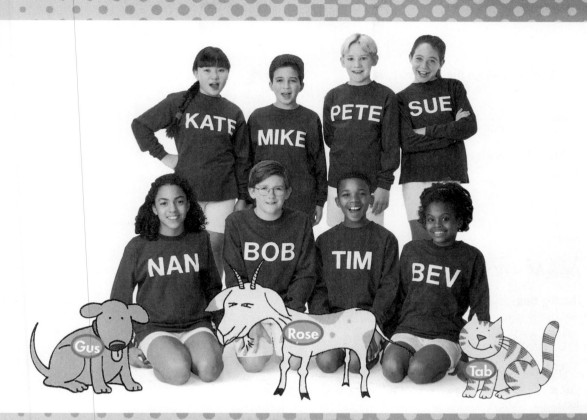

About the Authors

Kaye Wiley is an educator, curriculum developer, and writer with over twenty-eight years of classroom experience in the United States and abroad. She graduated from the University of California at Berkeley and completed an M.Ed. in Bilingual Education/ESL at the University of Houston, where she specialized in psycholinguistics and second language acquisition. After beginning her career in Concord, California, she went to Turkey, where she taught for ten years at the Istanbul Community School and Robert College. Then she returned to Houston, where she was head of ESL at Awty International School for nine years. Currently she is writing curriculum and teaching both ESL and foreign languages for the New Haven Public Schools in Connecticut. Kaye Wiley has written two previous books–*Alligator at the Airport* and *Animalito Alfabeto*–which also emphasize emerging literacy for new language learners.

Gary Apple is an experienced writer whose credits include works for children's television and the internet. He has contributed instructional material in the fields of reading, composition, ESL, and EFL. Gary Apple has a teacher's degree in Secondary English from the State University of New York at Brockport.

Contents

Introduction

Newcomer Phonics is a collection of brightly illustrated phonics activities designed to help new English language learners become confident, independent readers. The Student Book follows a careful progressive sequence, using high-frequency words in context--first with short vowels, then with long vowels, blends, digraphs, r-controlled vowels, and diphthongs. At the end of each phonics unit, there is also a humorous Little Book that students can remove, read to themselves, and take home for their own enjoyment.

THE TEACHER'S GUIDE

You may find that some older ELD students who can already decode in their own language will be able to proceed through the pages of **Newcomer Phonics** on their own, using the clearly illustrated examples. However, it is important to augment each lesson in the Student Book with specific oral language support from the Teacher's Guide, since students need to hear the spoken phonics sounds before they try to read them. Research shows us that the concept of sound-symbol linkage is developed most effectively through explicit phonics lessons and interactions between teachers and students. It is by listening and responding to the voice of the teacher that the students learn the variations in the English sound system, develop phonemic awareness, practice pronunciation, and build background in the language.

The Teacher's Guide provides not only step-by-step lessons and chants that strengthen this oral language connection, but also outlines suggestions for extension activities and assessments. The three-step lesson includes:

1. Developing Phonemic Awareness or Building Background

2. Using the Page instruction

3. Including All Learners activities for multiple learning styles that include informal oral and written assessments:

 and

Say It!   **Write It!**

DESCRIPTION OF THE PROGRAM

Q *How does Newcomer Phonics help students learning to read in English?*

A *Every word is illustrated.* More than 400 brightly illustrated nouns, verbs, and adjectives highlight the pages of the student book and provide visual support for new readers. Although some of these words will be familiar from conversation, ELD students often need visual cues to increase comprehension when decoding new words.

Only high-frequency words are used. For newcomers in English, certain words are more necessary to learn than others. *Bus* and *run,* for example, are more useful words to master when studying the short *u* sound than *jug* or *bun,* which students rarely encounter. In traditional phonics programs designed for native English speakers, there is often a "word-family" approach, using a wide array of low-frequency words. However, **Newcomer Phonics** uses only carefully selected, high-frequency vocabulary.

Words are presented in context, not in isolation. In contrast to traditional phonics programs that rely on lists of isolated words, **Newcomer Phonics** assumes that ELD students have a limited vocabulary base and need to derive meaning from context before they can complete exercises. Therefore, all new words are presented in relation to a picture, sentence, or story. In this way, there are three sets of cues to help newcomers decipher English text: (1) illustrations, which provide a visual context; (2) full sentences, which provide a verbal context; and (3) the characters of the Team, which provide a narrative context.

The vocabulary is highly controlled. Only words that have been previously introduced and illustrated are used in sentences and stories. Thus, as students come to the Little Books at the end of each phonics unit, they see familiar words and can feel the satisfaction of reading the story on their own. A word list of the controlled vocabulary is included in the Student Book.

Decodable text is used throughout. The units in **Newcomer Phonics** are carefully structured to emphasize the most frequent, highly regular sound-symbol relationships. It was the author's goal to make all the text as decodable as possible for ELD students. However, since some important words in English contain irregular sounds (*has* = /haz/, *who* = /hoo/), they are coded with a 🔑 and referenced on a pronunciation chart in the Student Book. Sight words like *the* are also referenced on this chart.

Phonics lessons progress systematically. Units are also designed to introduce ELD students to written English carefully, step-by-step. Whereas basic consonants will be familiar to many from similar sounds in their own language, English vowel sounds with their various pronunciations and spellings, as well as digraphs and diphthongs, may be new.

Syntax is simple, and language structures are limited.
Newcomers to English are at the early stages of language acquisition. They are progressing from silent listening to one-word utterances and short sentences. For this reason, activities and stories in **Newcomer Phonics** reinforce the following early-stage language structures:

1. Simple declarative sentences: *Nan has a hat.*

2. Present tense verbs: *go, see* (simple present tense); *is going, is seeing* (present progressive tense)

3. Negative forms: *Gus is not on the bus.*

4. Interrogative forms: *Is Gus on the bus?*

See the Scope and Sequence on pages viii -1 for more details.

Q How are Newcomer Phonics units organized?

A Words are repeated and recycled continually. At the end of each phonics unit there is a review page that helps students practice words from the given unit plus previous words from other units. In addition, recycling of vocabulary in the context of practice sentences continues throughout the book. The Little Books contain carefully controlled vocabulary that is cumulative as well, reviewing not only the words from the unit, but also words from prior units.

ELD thematic topics are included. To make the content of lessons more relevant for ELD students, phonics activities are designed around themes such as school, family, animals, house, clothes, sports, and weather. (See the Scope and Sequence on pages viii-1 for more details.)

Grammar topics are incorporated in exercises. Since older newcomers can sometimes benefit from a more structured approach to second-language learning, topics such as verbs, pronouns, prepositions, and adjectives are also included. Notes in the Teacher's Guide provide suggestions and extension activities for these grammatical topics.

Writing and reading are presented concurrently. In line with research suggesting that coding and decoding in language (i.e. reading and writing) reinforce each other when taught together, **Newcomer Phonics** includes writing opportunities in every unit. By learning phonics, ELD students are also practicing to write and spell with phonemes.

Q What are the "Little Books" ?

A At the end of each unit in the Student Book there is a pull-out page that can be folded in quarters to make small, colorful story books about the Phonics Team and their adventures. Students enjoy reading these Little Books to friends and family members and can keep them to start their own "library" in English.

Q What assessments does the program include?

A Newcomer Phonics includes both formal and informal assessments. The Student Book contains ten written assessment/review pages--a kind of mini-quiz at the end of each unit. The Teacher's Guide similarly contains twenty supplementary practice and written assessment pages. Equally important, however, are the ongoing informal assessments which the Student Book pages provide for the teacher and for students themselves, who can use them as self-assessments. The Teacher's Guide also contains oral and written assessments as part of each lesson plan.

Q What are the other components of the Newcomer Phonics program?

A Besides the Student Book and Teacher's Guide, there are two other valuable teaching aides in the **Newcomer Phonics** program: an audio program and colorful phonics cards.

Audio Program Over sixty lively chants, songs and the ten Little Book stories are recorded on an audiocassette and audio CD. These chants, songs, and stories recycle key vocabulary from the units and target the short vowels, long vowels, blends, digraphs, r-controlled vowels, and diphthongs in **Newcomer Phonics.**

Phonics Cards This set includes fifty 8 " X 10" two-sided cards (over ninety photographic and illustrated images), one for each phonic element taught in the program. Cards are categorized by ELD themes for more teaching opportunities and cross-classification. The teacher can cover words for assessment purposes.

Scope and Sequence

THE NEWCOMER PHONICS PROGRAM

	PHONIC ELEMENTS	GRAMMAR TOPICS	ELD THEMES
UNIT 1	short vowels: a, o, i, final x	verbs: *has, tap, jog, hop, can, cannot, sit, hit, is, is not;* prepositions: *on, off;* adjectives; possessives using *'s*	animals, household items, clothes, outdoors, sizes, emotions
UNIT 2	short vowels: u, e	verbs: *run, hug, has, get;* yes/no questions; plural *s*	outdoors, pets, bugs, colors, weather, numbers, transportation, parts of the body
UNIT 3	blends: cl, fl, pl, bl, gl, sl, gr, fr, br, tr, cr, dr, st, sp, sn, sw, sk, sm, lk, nd, mp, nk, ft, xt, st, sk, lp, lt, nt	verbs: *skip, spill, smell, swim, jump;* preposition: *next to*	school, outdoors, food, animals, transportation, weather, time, clothes, senses, colors
UNIT 4	long vowels: a	verbs: *make, take, wake, play, say, lay, wait, have;* contractions: *can't, isn't;* similar words	food, outdoor activities, landscape, animals, weather, time, emotions, face
UNIT 5	long vowels: i	verbs: *ride, like, fly, cry, glide, hide, bite;* pronouns: *I, my;* preposition: *by;* adjectives	recreation/bikes, numbers, time, parts of the body, day/night, left/right, rhymes, emotions, questions, lists, likes/dislikes

	PHONIC ELEMENTS	GRAMMAR TOPICS	ELD THEMES
UNIT 6	long vowels: o, e, u	verbs: *hold, float, grow, blow, read, sleep, eat, hear, see, use;* adjectives; pronouns: *he, me, you;* prepositions; *in back of, behind, beside, below, between, above, in front of;* questions with *do you;* contraction: *don't*	sports, games, weather, outdoors, temperature, plants, colors , animals, food, numbers, many/few, opposites, parts of the body, time, emotions, riddles, musical instruments
UNIT 7	digraphs: sh, ph, th	verbs: *wash, think, throw;* questions with *do you;* preposition: *with;* demonstrative pronouns and adjectives: *this, that, these, those*	transportation, telephone, clothes, bathing, animals, parts of the body, math, graphs, outdoor activities, rhymes
UNIT 8	digraphs: wh, ng, ch, tch, wr, kn	verbs: *sing, catch, watch, pitch, write, know;* questions with *what;* questions with *when;* adjectives; present progressive verbs; homonyms	weather, animals, numbers, time, school, healthy habits, safety, months, lunch, math, utensils, outdoors, thinking/ imagining, sports, songs, right/wrong, riddles, rhymes
UNIT 9	r-controlled vowels: ar, er, ir, ur	prepositions: *over/under, before/after*	farm, outdoors, weather, seasons, family, clothes, colors, parts of the body, safety, animals, time, transportation, numbers
UNIT 10	diphthongs: oo, ou, ow, oy, oi	verbs: *shoot, bounce;* adjectives; preposition: *around;* questions with *how*	house, rooms, town, noises, school, toys, sports, games, animals, animal sounds, onomatopoeia, musical sounds, riddles, parts of the body, colors, exclamations, parties/celebrations

UNIT 1

Short Vowels: a, o, i

Short Vowels: /a/ a

Key Words: Nan, has, cat, map, hat, bag, pan, man, mat, van, tap, Tab, fat

---

Phonics Objectives

Can students:
- ✓ listen for /a/ as in *Nan?*
- ✓ identify the short vowel sound the letter *a* stands for?
- ✓ read and write the letter *a* in words and sentences?

Language Acquisition Objectives

Students:
- use the verbs *has, tap*

ESL Standards

- Goal 2, Standard 1

UNIT 1 Short Vowels: a, o, i   **a Nan**

Nan has a cat.   map   hat   bag   pan

Match the sentences with the pictures.

1. Nan has a cat.
2. Nan has a map.
3. Nan has a hat.
4. Nan has a bag.
5. Nan has a pan.

a b c d e

2 Unit 1
Short Vowels: /a/ a; Verb: has

DEVELOPING PHONEMIC AWARENESS

Point out and pronounce objects in the class that have the short *a* sound such as a *map,* a *hat,* a book *bag,* and your *hand.* Say the word *map* and model oral blending: *mmmmaaaaaap.* Invite students to practice slowly blending the sounds in the words with you. Then ask them to tell you how the words are alike. (/a/ *sound*)

Display pictures of objects such as a *pan,* a *cat,* a *mat,* a *man,* Nan, and a *van.* Pass these around and ask students to say their names. Listen to students' pronunciation and correct them, asking them to repeat the word if necessary.

Say the following words and ask students to clap when they hear a word with the short *a* sound: *hop, nap, hill, sat, sit, bag,* and *ball.*

USING THE PAGES

Page 2

Ask students to:
- point to letter *a* that stands for /a/
- listen as you read words in box
- locate words as you repeat them
- read aloud and track words with you

Direct students' attention to the box at the top of the page. Read aloud the sentence *Nan has a cat.* Point out the pronunciation key icon under the word *has.* Explain that students can look up the pronunciation of any words that appear with this icon by referring to the key at the end of their Student Books.

Point out the photo of Nan on page 3 and the illustrations of Nan on pages 2–3. Explain that each Phonics Team character appears both in photos and cartoons.

Page 3

Ask students to:
- point to letter *a* that stands for /a/
- listen as you read words in box
- locate words as you repeat them
- read aloud and track words with you

Read together: *"Nan has. . . ."* Ask a student to role-play Nan. Give her a hat and say, *Nan has a hat.* Give another student a bag and say, *(name of student) has a bag, Nan has a hat.* Switch objects and ask the class, *Who has a hat? Who has a bag?* You can continue the activity with other short *a* objects and students.

Read the sentence *Nan taps a bag* and demonstrate the verb *taps* by tapping a finger on something.

Point out *Tab, the fat cat,* as an illustration in the top box and photo on page 2.

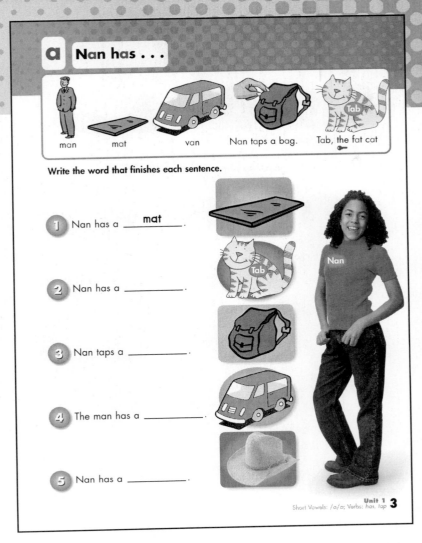

a | **Nan has . . .**

man mat van Nan taps a bag. Tab, the fat cat

Write the word that finishes each sentence.

1. Nan has a ___mat___ .

2. Nan has a _____ .

3. Nan taps a _____ .

4. The man has a _____ .

5. Nan has a _____ .

INCLUDING ALL LEARNERS

Play a "Grab Bag" Game
(Kinesthetic Learners)

Materials: a large bag made of paper, plastic, or cloth, small objects that have a short *a* in the middle of their names, such as a toy *van*, a little *fan*, a *map*, a *hat*, a *pan*, and a toy *cat*.

Emphasize the short *a* sound as you explain what a *grab bag* is.

Ask students to take turns pulling out objects from the bag and naming them. Give them the opportunity to find other objects in the room to add to the bag. Each time the object is named, students can gain a point. As a student pulls out an object, ask the other players to say: *(Lin) has a map. (Maria) has a van.*

Make a Collage
(Visual Learners)

Materials: construction paper, old magazines, scissors, glue, crayons or markers

Ask students to draw pictures of short *a* objects they know. They may also want to include cutouts of short *a* words from magazines and design a collage by pasting them, along with their drawings, on paper. Have students tell you or a partner the short *a* objects they put into their collage.

Sing a Short *a* Song
(Auditory Learners)

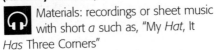 Materials: recordings or sheet music with short *a* such as, "My *Hat*, It *Has* Three Corners"

> My hat, it has three corners,
> Three corners has my hat,
> And had it not three corners,
> It would not be my hat.

Play a tape or an instrument to accompany a song with a short *a*. Invite students to make a list of popular songs they know that use words with short *a*. Sing the songs with students and record their voices. Replay the songs to celebrate their learning of the first short vowel.

Find That Cat in the Hat!
(Extra Help)

Materials: trade books that have short *a* words in the title: *The Cat in the Hat, Cat Traps, Batman*

Invite students to read the titles of these books aloud. Ask them to begin a list of short *a* titles in their journals or writing portfolios. Read the books aloud and then give them opportunities to practice reading the books together.

Say It!

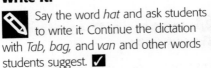 Make up short rhymes, raps, or jingles with lots of short *a*'s, such as the following.

> Nan has a cat, cat, cat.
> Nan has a cat, cat, cat.
> Nan has a cat, cat, cat.
> Nan has a cat named Tab.

Say the jingle aloud. Model orally blending the words, such as: *Nnnnaaaaaan.* Ask students to listen for the short *a* sound and tell you in which words they hear it. ✔

Write It!

Say the word *hat* and ask students to write it. Continue the dictation with *Tab, bag,* and *van* and other words students suggest. ✔

Short Vowels: /o/ o

Key Words: Bob, jog, hop, dog, doll, on, off, rock, pot, can, cannot

Phonics Objectives

Can students:
- ✓ listen for /o/ as in *Bob?*
- ✓ identify the short vowel sound the letter *o* stands for?
- ✓ read and write the letter *o* in words and sentences?

Language Acquisition Objectives

Can students:
- ✓ use the verbs *jog, hop, can cannot?*

Students:
- use the prepositions *on, off*

ESL Standards

- Goal 1, Standard 3

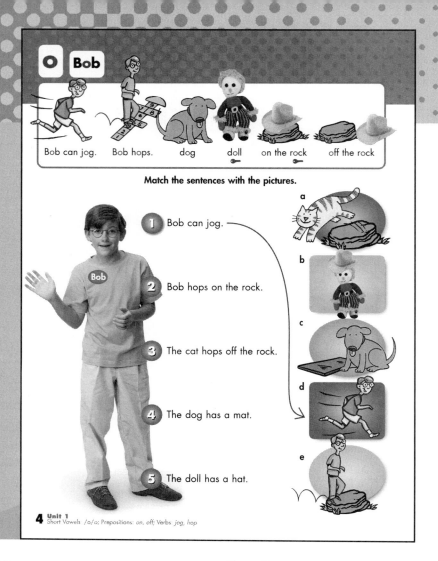

o Bob

Bob can jog.   Bob hops.   dog   doll   on the rock   off the rock

Match the sentences with the pictures.

Bob

1. Bob can jog.
2. Bob hops on the rock.
3. The cat hops off the rock.
4. The dog has a mat.
5. The doll has a hat.

a
b
c
d
e

4 Unit 1
Short Vowels /o/o; Prepositions: *on, off*; Verbs: *jog, hop*

DEVELOPING PHONEMIC AWARENESS

Display a collection of three or four objects that have the short *o* sound in them. These may include a *rock,* a *doll,* a stuffed *dog,* and a *top.* Lift each item and pronounce its name for the students. Model oral blending. For example, say the word *rock: rrrroooock.* Invite students to pronounce the words after you. Then ask the students to tell you how the names for the items are alike. *(/o/ sound)*

Keeping the short *o* objects on display, add a few other items that do not have the short *o* sound. In a random order, pick up the items one at a time. Challenge the students to clap their hands when you lift an item that has the short *o* sound.

USING THE PAGES

Page 4

Ask students to:
- point to letter *o* that stands for /o/
- listen as you read words in box
- locate words as you repeat them
- read aloud and track words with you

Ask students to look at the sentence *Bob can jog* and its illustration in the box. Read the sentence aloud and demonstrate the verb *jog.* Then point to the sentence *Bob hops* with its illustration, read it aloud, and demonstrate the verb *hops.*

Direct students' attention to the illustrations of the hat on the rock and the hat off the rock in the box. Then demonstrate the prepositions *on* and *off* with objects in the class.

Page 5

Ask students to:
- point to letter *o* that stands for /o/
- listen as you read words in box
- locate words as you repeat them
- read aloud and track words with you

Point out the words *can* and *cannot* at the top of the page and ask the class to repeat them after you. Ask, *Which word has the short o sound?*

Request that a student stand up and hop. Say, *(Name) can hop.* Invite the class to repeat the sentence. Next, ask the student to fly. Say, *(Name of student) cannot fly.* Have the class repeat the sentence. You can repeat this with other actions that students can and cannot do.

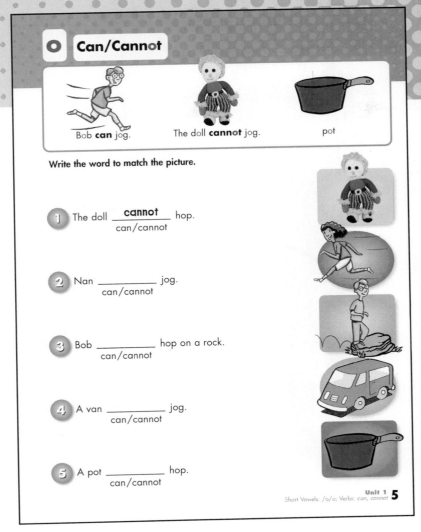

○ Can/Cannot

Bob **can** jog.　　The doll **cannot** jog.　　pot

Write the word to match the picture.

1. The doll __cannot__ hop.
   can/cannot

2. Nan _____ jog.
   can/cannot

3. Bob _____ hop on a rock.
   can/cannot

4. A van _____ jog.
   can/cannot

5. A pot _____ hop.
   can/cannot

Short Vowels: /o/ o; Verbs: can, cannot **5**

sary, help individual students think of appropriate items. When they are finished, hand the shopping basket to a volunteer. Ask him or her to go around the room and "shop" for three items, saying the name of the item as he or she drops it in the basket. Allow other students to take turns shopping.

Say It!

Teach students the following chant. 🎧

> I can hop. Hop, hop, hop!
> I can jog. Jog, jog, jog!
> I can mop. Mop, mop, mop.
> I can spin like a top, top, top.

Call on students to find the words with the short *o* sound. Choose some words to model orally blending the sounds together, such as: *hhhhoooooop*. As the class performs the chant, challenge them to perform the actions indicated. ✔

Write It!

On the chalkboard, write the following two sentences:

I can _____.

A van cannot _____.

Ask students to think of two short *o* words to complete the sentences and then write the sentences. ✔

INCLUDING ALL LEARNERS

Spin Like a Top
(Kinesthetic Learners)

Materials: pictures of objects that have the short *o* sound in their name (i.e. *top, mop, rock, pot*), pictures of objects that do not have the short *o* sound, a paper bag

Write the word *top* on the chalkboard and pronounce it for the class, stressing the short *o* sound. Ask the students to say the word as they spin like a top.

Let students take turns pulling pictures out of the bag and naming them. If a picture has the short *o* sound, they should spin like a top after they say the word.

Stop the Train
(Auditory/Kinesthetic Learners)

Write the word *stop* on the chalkboard. Pronounce it for the class, stressing the short *o* sound. Have students repeat it after you.

Invite students to form a line and ask them to imagine they are cars in a train. Tell them that you are going to read a list of words as the "train" moves around the classroom. When they hear a word with the short *o* sound in it, the train should stop. Instruct the train to move as you begin saying words, some of which should have the short *o* sound in them. (These may include *hop, shop, top, jog, slot, pot.*)You may want to have students take turns being the lead train car.

Let's Shop
(Visual Learners)

Materials: drawing paper, crayons or markers, a shopping basket or shopping bag

Write the word *shop* on the chalkboard and say it aloud for the class. Tell students that they are going on a shopping trip.

Distribute the drawing materials. Ask students to draw a picture of an object with the short *o* sound in its name. If neces-

Short Vowels: /i/ *i*

Key Words: Tim, sit, hill, hit, is, mitt, big, little

Phonics Objectives

Can students:
- ✓ listen for /i/ as in *Tim*?
- ✓ identify the sound the letter *i* stands for?
- ✓ read and write the letter *i* in words and sentences?

Language Acquisition Objectives

Students:
- use the verbs *sit, hit, is*
- use the adjectives *big, little, sad, mad, hot*
- complete sentences using *is/is not* + an adjective

ESL Standards

- Goal 1, Standard 1

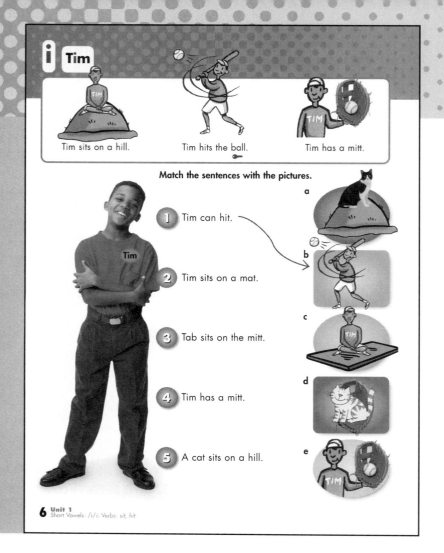

Match the sentences with the pictures.

1. Tim can hit.
2. Tim sits on a mat.
3. Tab sits on the mitt.
4. Tim has a mitt.
5. A cat sits on a hill.

6 Unit 1
Short Vowels: /i/ i; Verbs: *sit, hit*

DEVELOPING PHONEMIC AWARENESS

Point to your chin and say the word *chin*. Ask students to point to their own chins and repeat *chin* after you. Hand each student a piece of scrap paper. Take a piece of paper and say the word *rip*, then rip the paper. Ask the students to rip their own pieces of paper as they say the word *rip*. Tell them to blend slowly the sounds in *rip* together: *rrrriiiip.* Ask students to listen to the sound they hear in the middle of *chin* and *rip*.

Say the following words and ask students to rip small pieces of paper when they hear a word with the short *i* sound in it: *top, tip, pot, pit, mitt, has, his, at, is.*

USING THE PAGES

Page 6

Ask students to:
- point to letter *i* that stands for /i/
- listen as you read words in box
- locate words as you repeat them
- read aloud and track words with you

Invite the class to examine the illustrations in the box. Point to the sentence *Tim sits on a hill* and read it aloud. Ask, *Which three words have the /i/ sound? (Tim, sits, hill)* Repeat this activity with the other two sentences in the box. Ask a volunteer to demonstrate the verb *sit* and another volunteer to pretend to *hit* a ball with a bat.

Page 7

Ask students to:
- point to letter *i* that stands for /i/
- listen as you read words in box
- locate words as you repeat them
- read aloud and track words with you

Pronounce the words *is* and *is not* and invite the class to repeat them after you. Ask the class to look at the first picture in the box. Read the first phrase *is big* and ask students to point to the picture of the big dog as they say *is big* after you. Repeat this with the phrase *is not big* and the little dog. Repeat with the other three pairs of illustrations in the box.

i | Is/Is Not

is sad/is not sad

is hot/is not hot

is big/is not big (little)

is mad/is not mad

Write the word or words to match the picture.

1. Tim ___**is**___ mad.
   is/is not

2. The pan _____ hot.
   is/is not

3. The van _____ big.
   is/is not

4. Nan _____ sad.
   is/is not

5. The cat _____ big.
   is/is not

Short Vowels: /i/i; Verbs: is, is not; Adjectives **Unit 1 7**

Distribute the magazines, newspapers, and scissors. Challenge the students to find and cut out pictures of pairs of items that are big and little (examples: a big dog and a small dog, a big truck and a small truck). When they are done, invite the students to pin their pictures on the appropriate column on the bulletin board.

Say It!

Teach the class the following rhyme. 🎧

> On the hill, on the hill
> sits Bill, sits Bill.
> Is it Tim, is it Tim
> with him, with him?

Call on students to tell you the words with the short *i* sound. Invite volunteers to model blending the sounds in the words. After the class recites the rhyme, you can extend the activity by helping the students come up with additional stanzas. ✔

Write It!

Write the above chant on the chalkboard. Then ask students to copy the chant onto paper and circle all the words with the short *i* sound. ✔

INCLUDING ALL LEARNERS

Simon Says Short *i*
(Kinesthetic/Auditory Learners)

Ask the class to stand. Tell them to listen very carefully as you say different action words: *jog, sit, tap, has, hit a ball, hop, spin*. If the word you say has the short *i* sound, they should pretend to do the action. If the word you say does not have the short *i* sound, they should keep still. If students move when you say a word that does not have the *i* sound, they must sit out and stop playing the game. Continue until only one student is standing. You can make the game more difficult by asking students to repeat each word after you.

Hit It
(Kinesthetic Learners)

Materials: pictures for words with and without the short *i* sound

Invite a pair of students to play a game. Have them stand face to face on either side of a desk. Tell them that you are going to put a card on the desk and say its name. If the word has the short *i* sound in it, the students should race to slap their hand over the card. The student who gets there first gets one point. If a student slaps a card that does not have the short *i* sound, he or she loses a point. When all the cards have been used, the student with the most points is the winner. Repeat with other pairs of students. To make this game more difficult, do not say the name of the picture. Instead, ask the student who slaps the card to say its name. He or she gets a point only if the word is pronounced correctly.

Big and Little
(Extra Help)

Materials: old magazines and newspapers, scissors

Divide a bulletin board into two sections labeled *BIG* and *LITTLE*. Read the words for the students, stressing the short *i* sound. Invite the class to repeat the words after you.

Short Vowels: /a/ a, /o/ o, /i/ i

Key Words: of, on, off

The bag of Tim = Tim's bag

Match the sentences that mean the same thing.

1. The hat **of Tim** is not big.
2. The cat **of Nan** is on the mat.
3. The bag **of Tim** is big.
4. The dog **of Bob** can jog.

a. **Tim's** bag is big.
b. **Nan's** cat is on the mat.
c. **Bob's** dog can jog.
d. **Tim's** hat is not big.

On/Off

Write the word to match the picture.

1. Nan's hat is ___**on**___ the dog.
   on/off

2. Tab is _____ the mat.
   on/off

3. Bob is _____ the rock.
   on/off

8 Unit 1
Short Vowels:/a/a, /o/o, Possessives; Prepositions: on, off

BUILDING BACKGROUND

Ask a student to come forward. Hand him or her a bag and say, *This is (student's name)'s bag.* Ask the student to hand the bag to another child and repeat the phrase, using that child's name.

Then place a piece of paper on the floor. Stand on it and say, *I am standing on the paper.* Step off the paper and say, *I am off the paper.* Invite students to perform *on* and *off* movements in front of the class.

USING PAGE 8

Read and track *The bag of Tim* and *Tim's bag* at the top of the page. Explain that both phrases mean the same thing: *The bag belongs to Tim.* Point to the apostrophe in the second phrase and explain how *'s* indicates that something belongs to someone or something else.

Ask a volunteer to point to the picture that shows the hat *on* the rock. Let another volunteer point to the picture of the hat *off* the rock.

INCLUDING ALL LEARNERS

Whose Is It?
(Kinesthetic Learners)

Invite volunteers to hold up something they own. Write the corresponding pairs of phrases on the chalkboard, such as *the book of Lynn = Lynn's book.*

Say It!

Materials: a hat

Ask a volunteer to stand up. Hold up the hat and say, *This is (name of student)'s hat.* Place the hat on the student's head and then say, *The hat is on (name of student)'s head.* Ask the volunteer to go to

another student and do and say the same things. (Example: *This is Tina's hat. The hat is on Tina's head.*) Repeat the activity with other volunteers. ✓

Write It!

Write the following on the board and ask students to fill in the blanks with the correct word(s):

The ball of Tim = _____

_____ = Bob's bag

The doll of Nan = _____ ✓

Little Book: *The Big Bag*

Key Words: big, bag, Nan, has, hat, map, tap, hop, cannot, is, Tab, mat, mad

Phonics Objectives

Can students:
- ✓ listen for the /a/ as in *Nan*, /o/ as in *hop*, and /i/ as in *big*?
- ✓ read letters for short vowels *a*, *o*, and *i* in words in the context of a story?
- ✓ write words with the short vowels *a, o,* and *i?*

Language Acquisition Objectives

Can students:
- ✓ read words in story context?

ESL Standards

- Goal 1, Standard 2

DEVELOPING PHONEMIC AWARENESS

Invite students to listen as you recite (or play) the chant below. Ask them to listen carefully for the short vowel sounds /a/, /o/, and /i/.

> Nan, Nan
> Has a cat, cat.
> Nan, Nan
> Has a fat cat.
> Nan, Nan
> Has a fat cat
> In her big bag
> IN HER BIG BAG?

Invite students to recite the chant with you and then as a group on their own. Model orally blending sounds in words from the chant, such as: *ffffaaaaaat.* Listen to students slowly saying words as they blend the sounds. Let students tell you which words contain the short vowel sounds they have learned.

USING THE LITTLE BOOK

Explain to the students that they are going to make a Little Book about Nan. Ask them to remove pages 9 and 10 from their books. Show them how to cut the page on the dotted line with the scissors icon, then fold the pieces to make their own eight-page Little Book.

Preview *The Big Bag* by reading the title aloud. Allow the students time to look through the book and examine the pictures. Ask students to follow along as you read the story aloud to them, tracking the words. Then read the story together as a group.

Engage the class in the story. You can prompt the discussion by asking questions that bring in their own personal experiences and opinions, such as *Do you have any pets? Have your pets or animals ever done anything that made you laugh?*

Revisit the story. Lead the class in a second reading of *The Big Bag*. This time, ask for volunteers to read aloud one page at a time. After each page is read, ask questions focusing on the content of the story. Here are some examples:

- *Who has a big bag?*
- *What is in the bag?*
- *Why does the bag hop?*

INCLUDING ALL LEARNERS

Act Out the Story: *The Big Bag*
(Kinesthetic/Auditory Learners)

Materials: a large book bag, a hat, a road map, a stuffed toy cat

Place the hat, map, and toy cat in the book bag. Tell the class that they are going to act out the story *The Big Bag*. Ask for a volunteer to play Nan. Have the volunteer act out the story as you read it aloud to the class. When you are done, ask for a pair of volunteers—one to play Nan and the other to read the story aloud. Encourage other pairs of volunteers to perform the story for the class.

Story Time
(Extra Help)

Materials: photocopy of *The Big Bag*, scissors, large index cards, tape

Cut out the pages of *The Big Bag* and mount them on the index cards. (When you are through, you'll have some "text cards" and some "picture cards.")

Place the title card and the picture cards on the chalk rail, leaving spaces between them. Hold up the first text card and read it for the class. Ask a volunteer to place the card beside the picture it describes. Continue until all the pages are used. You can vary the activity by placing the text cards on the chalk rail and handing students picture cards.

Say It!

Read the story aloud again and have students clap each time they hear you say words with the short *a, o, i* sounds. Pick words from the story and ask volunteers to pronounce the sounds in each word, then blend them together. ✓

Nan has a big bag.
The bag has a hat in it.
The bag has a map in it.

Nan taps the bag.
The bag hops.
A bag cannot hop!

Write It!

 Ask students to look at their Little Books and write down a list of all the words that have short *a, o, i* sounds. Have students go over their lists with partners. ✓

Family Connection

Send home the Little Book *The Big Bag*. Encourage students to read the book to a family member.

BOOK CORNER

/a/ *a*
The Cat in the Hat by Dr. Seuss

/a/ *a*, /i/ *i*
Millions of Cats by Wanda Gag

/o/ *o*
Mop Top by Don Freeman

/o/ *o*
Hop on Pop by Dr. Seuss

/i/ *i*
Clifford, the Big Red Dog by Norman Bridwell

/i/ *i*
Bit by Bit by Steve Sanfield

Review

Short Vowels: *a, o, i*
Introduction: Final *x*

Key Words: fox, box, six, ax, socks

Phonics Objectives

Can students:

✓ listen for and identify /a/, /o/, /i/, /ks/?

✓ read and write the letters for short vowels *a, o, i,* and final *x* in words and sentences?

Language Acquisition Objectives

Students:

• respond to statements with *yes* or *no*

• use verbs *has, is*

ESL Standards

• Goal 2, Standard 1

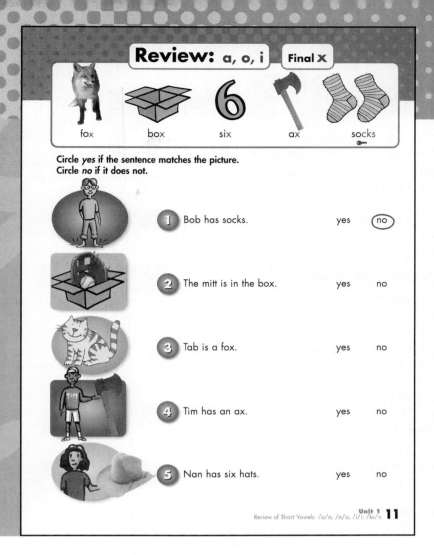

Review: a, o, i **Final X**

fox	box	six	ax	socks

Circle *yes* if the sentence matches the picture.
Circle *no* if it does not.

1. Bob has socks. yes (no)
2. The mitt is in the box. yes no
3. Tab is a fox. yes no
4. Tim has an ax. yes no
5. Nan has six hats. yes no

Review of Short Vowels: /a/a, /o/o, /i/i, /ks/x **Unit 1** **11**

DEVELOPING PHONEMIC AWARENESS

Introduce final *x* by displaying a cardboard box. Have students say the word together with you. Then say these words and ask children to clap when they hear a word that ends like *box: fox, mop, ax, six, ox, Tim.* Encourage them to think of other words that end with the same sound.

Ask a student wearing socks to come forward. Point out that the child is wearing socks and say, *(name of student) has socks.* Ask students to listen to the words *socks* and *box.* Say the words and model oral blending: *sssssooooocks, boooox.* Point out that they end with the same sound.

USING THE REVIEW PAGE

Ask students to:
• point to letters *a, o, i, x* that stand for /a/, /o/, /i/, /ks/
• listen as you read words in box
• locate words as you repeat them
• read aloud and track words with you

Point to the letter *a* at the top of the page. Invite a volunteer to identify the letter and the sound. Do the same for the letters *o* and *i.* Then point to *Final x.* Explain that *x* is a letter that often appears at the end of words after short vowels such as *a, o,* and *i.*

Pronounce the words with final *x* in the box: *box, six, ax. Which sound is the same for all three words?* (/ks/) Pronounce the word *socks* and ask students to repeat it. Point out that the letters *cks* make the same sound as final *x.*

INCLUDING ALL LEARNERS

Yes or No?
(Auditory Learners)

Divide the class into pairs or small groups. Have students take turns making up and reading aloud sentences with *yes/no* answers.

Say It!

Play a game with students by placing them in pairs and asking them to create sentences using words that end in final *x,* such as *The fox sat on the box,* or *Max has an ax.* List their ideas on the board. ✓

Write It!

Ask students to write the words that end in *x* as you say them: *fox, box, ox, six, ax.* Encourage them to add words that they know that end in *x,* such as *fax.* ✓

UNIT 2

Short Vowels: u, e

Short Vowels: /u/ u

Key Words: Gus, run, bus, up, bug, hug, fun, tub, nut, rug, sun

Phonics Objectives

Can students:
- ✓ listen for /u/ as in *Gus*?
- ✓ identify the short vowel sound the letter *u* stands for?
- ✓ read and write the letter *u* in words and sentences?

Language Acquisition Objectives

Students:
- use the verbs *run, hug, has*

ESL Standards

- Goal 2, Standard 1

DEVELOPING PHONEMIC AWARENESS

Say the word *up* as you point upward and jump up in front of the class. Ask the class to jump up as they say the word *up* with you. Now say the words *up* and *bug* modelling oral blending: *uuuup, buuuug.* Ask, *What do the words* up *and* bug *have in common?* (/u/ *sound*)

Tell the class that you are going to say a series of words. When the students hear a word with the short *u* sound, they should jump up. You may wish to use the following list of words: *bag, tip, hug, run, tub, pop, sun.*

To extend this activity, randomly display pictures for words with and without the short *u* sound. When students see a picture with a name that has the short *u* sound, they should say the word and jump up.

USING THE PAGES

Page 12

Ask students to:
- point to letter *u* that stands for /u/
- listen as you read words in box
- locate words as you repeat them
- read aloud and track words with you

Point to the sentence *Gus can run* and read it aloud for the students. Ask them to repeat the sentence after you. Ask a volunteer to demonstrate the verb *run* by running in place. Then point out the sentence *Nan hugs Gus* and the illustration that shows this action.

If possible, bring in a jack-in-the-box to show students a real model of a jack-in-the-box, which is the subject of sentence 4. Bringing in real-life items to illustrate words and actions will add fun and immediacy to class activities.

Page 13

Ask students to:
- point to letter *u* that stands for /u/
- listen as you read words in box
- locate words as you repeat them
- read aloud and track words with you

Read the sentence *Gus has fun* aloud and invite the class to repeat it after you. Ask students what they like to do to have *fun*.

Display a toy plastic bug or another small item with a short *u* sound. Hand the bug to one of your students and say, *(student's name) has the bug.* Invite the class to repeat the sentence. Ask that student to hand the bug to a classmate and say, *(new student's name) has the bug.* Have students pass the toy bug and say the sentence until everyone has had a turn.

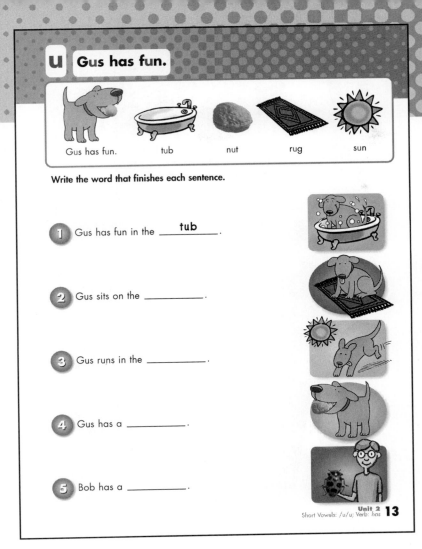

u | **Gus has fun.**

Gus has fun.   tub   nut   rug   sun

Write the word that finishes each sentence.

1   Gus has fun in the _____tub_____.

2   Gus sits on the _____.

3   Gus runs in the _____.

4   Gus has a _____.

5   Bob has a _____.

INCLUDING ALL LEARNERS

Hop on the Bus
(Kinesthetic/Auditory Learners)

This game is played like Musical Chairs. Arrange pairs of classroom chairs and tell the class that they are seats on a bus. Make sure that there is one less chair than there are students playing the game.

Ask the players to walk around the "bus" and listen as you read words. When they hear a word with the short *u* sound, they must try to get a seat on the bus. The student who is left without a seat is out of the game. Remove a chair from the bus and repeat until only one student is left on the bus.

Fill the Tub
(Visual Learners)

Materials: small tub or bucket, construction paper, crayons or markers

Bring in a small tub or bucket and say its name for the students, pointing out the short *u* sound. Distribute drawing materials to the students and ask them to draw pictures of objects with the short *u* sound. If necessary, help the students come up with appropriate objects such as *bug, sun, rug,* and *pup*. When they are finished drawing, invite the students to come up one at a time and drop their drawing in the tub or bucket, saying the name of their drawing as they do. You may extend the activity by inviting students to randomly pull pictures out of the tub or bucket and naming them.

Fun in the Sun
(Extra Help)

Materials: old magazines and newspapers, old advertisements, yellow construction paper, paste, scissors

Distribute the yellow construction paper and ask students to cut out the shape of the sun. (You may wish to provide a sun on cardboard for them to trace.) Then, ask students to look through the magazines and find a picture of something they think is fun. Tell them to cut out the picture and paste it on the sun they made. Point out that both the words *sun* and *fun* have the short *u* sound. When they are finished, invite volunteers to share their work.

Say It!

Teach the class this two-part choral chant to say with you. 🎧

Teacher: There's a bug,
              There's a bug,
              There's a bug on the rug!

Class: Oh no!

Teacher: In the tub
              In the tub
              There's a bug in the tub!

Class: Oh no!

Call on students to find the words with the short *u* sounds. Invite volunteers to model blending the sounds in the words. After the class recites the chant, you can switch parts. ✓

Write It!

Distribute writing paper to each student. One at a time, display pictures for the short *u* words. Ask the students to write down the word for each picture. Review the work as a class. ✓

Short Vowels: /e/ e

Key Words: Bev, pen, bed, red, get, bell, pet, men, seven, leg

Phonics Objectives

Can students:
- ✓ listen for /e/ as in *Bev?*
- ✓ identify the short vowel sound the letter *e* stands for?
- ✓ read and write the letter *e* in words and sentences?

Language Acquisition Objectives

Students:
- use verbs to begin question sentences
- use the verb *get*

ESL Standards

- Goal 1, Standard 3

DEVELOPING PHONEMIC AWARENESS

Hold up a red pen and say, *red pen*, stressing the short *e* sound. Model blending the sounds in the words together: *rrrreeeed peeeennnn*. Invite the class to repeat it after you.

Make sure that each student has a pen. Tell them that you are going to read some words aloud. If the word has the short *e* sound, they are to tap their pens. Read a list of words, some of which have the short *e* sound, such as *bug, ten, hot, hit, red, pen, men, cat, seven,* and *test*.

To extend this activity, randomly display pictures for words with and without the short *e* sound. When the students see a picture with a name that has the short *e* sound, they can say the word and tap their pens.

USING THE PAGES

Page 14

Ask students to:
- point to letter *e* that stands for /e/
- listen as you read words in box
- locate words as you repeat them
- read aloud and track words with you

Point to the phrases *get on the bus* and *get off the bus*. Ask students what other things they *get on* and *get off*. Use the new key words and words they already know to make up new sentences. (Example: *Bev gets on a red bus. Bev has a red bed.*) Write these new sentences on the board and track the words as you read them aloud to the students.

Page 15

Ask students to:
- point to letter *e* that stands for /e/
- listen as you read words in box
- locate words as you repeat them
- read aloud and track words with you

Read *Is Bev . . . ?* aloud and have the class repeat it after you. Explain that this is the beginning of a question. Suggest a few words that may complete the question. (*Is Bev a bug?*) Invite volunteers to provide other words that could complete the question.

Read the first word *bell* aloud and ask students to point to a magazine picture of a bell, or a real bell, if you have one. Repeat this with the other short *e* words in the box.

e Is Bev . . . ?

bell   pets   men   seven   leg

Circle *yes* or *no* to answer the questions.

1. Is Bev's leg up?   yes   (no)

2. Is Bev in a van?   yes   no

3. Can Bev's doll run?   yes   no

4. Can the pets run?   yes   no

5. Can seven men jog?   yes   no

Short Vowels: /e/e; Yes/No questions **Unit 2 15**

INCLUDING ALL LEARNERS

Write a Red Word
(Kinesthetic/Auditory Learners)

Materials: white chalk, red markers, sack, magazine pictures of short *e* words on index cards

Display pictures of short *e* words. Put ten pieces of white chalk and five red markers in a sack.

Write the word *red* on the easel paper and point out the short *e* sound. Ask a volunteer to reach into the sack and pick out a piece of chalk or marker at random. If the student picks a white piece of chalk, he or she can write any word already learned on the chalkboard. However, if the student selects a marker, he or she must write a word that matches one of the magazine pictures. Remove that picture, then continue the activity until all the pictures have been used.

Plenty of Tens
(Visual Learners)

Materials: drawing paper, magazines and newspapers

On the chalkboard, write short *e* words such as *leg, pet, men, bell,* and *bed.* Divide the class into pairs or small groups. Tell students that they're going to draw ten items that have the short *e* sound in their names. Ask pairs of students to look around the room for items. Provide magazines and newspapers for ideas. Set a timer or stop watch. When they are finished with their short *e* collections, invite the groups to label, display, and describe their work to the rest of the class.

Ed and Ned and Ted
(Extra Help)

Materials: telephone directories

Write the name *Bev* on the chalkboard and point out the short *e* sound. Remind the class that *Bev* is a name. Brainstorm with the class other names that have the short *e* sound in them. Some suggestions might be *Ted, Ned, Ed, Fred, Seth, Tess, Nell,* and *Kevin.* Write the names on the chalkboard. Divide the class into pairs or small groups and distribute telephone directories. Challenge the students to find full names of people that include the short *e* names that are on the chalkboard. When they are finished, invite the groups to present their findings to the rest of the class.

Say It!

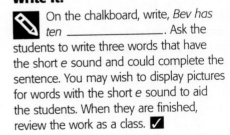 Teach the class the following two-part chant. Divide the class in two and have half the class say the sentences, and the other half say the numbers and clap. Then switch.

> Bev has ten pets.
> Ten!
> Ted has seven.
> Seven!
> Ed has two pets.
> Two!
> And so does Sue.
> (clap, clap)
> How about you?
> (clap, clap) ✓

Write It!

On the chalkboard, write, *Bev has ten _____.* Ask the students to write three words that have the short *e* sound and could complete the sentence. You may wish to display pictures for words with the short *e* sound to aid the students. When they are finished, review the work as a class. ✓

Short Vowels: /a/ a, /o/ o, /i/ i, /u/ u, /e/ e

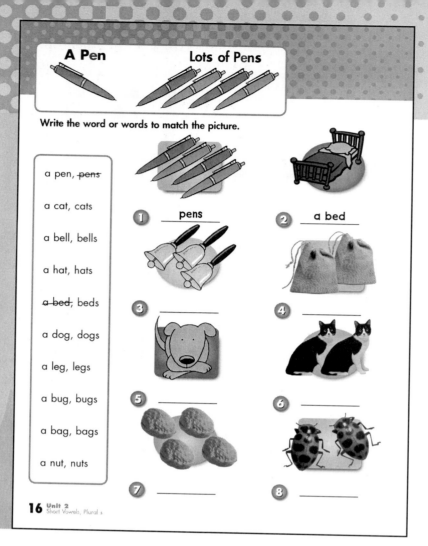

A Pen **Lots of Pens**

Write the word or words to match the picture.

- a pen, ~~pens~~
- a cat, cats
- a bell, bells
- a hat, hats
- ~~a bed~~, beds
- a dog, dogs
- a leg, legs
- a bug, bugs
- a bag, bags
- a nut, nuts

1. pens
2. a bed
3.
4.
5.
6.
7.
8.

Phonics Objectives

Can students:
- ✓ listen for /a/, /o/, /i/, /u/, and /e/?
- ✓ identify the short vowel sounds the letters *a, o, i, u,* and *e* stand for?
- ✓ read and write the letters *a, o, i, u,* and *e* in words and sentences?

Language Acquisition Objectives

Can students:
- ✓ add *s* to form plurals?

ESL Standards
- Goal 1, Standard 1

BUILDING BACKGROUND

Ask for three volunteers to come to the front of the class. Separate the group of three students into two students and one student. Write the words *student* and *students* on the chalkboard. Draw simple picture rebuses to represent the words. Point to the one student with one finger saying, *one student,* and to the two students with two fingers saying, *two students.* Emphasize the final /s/ sound in *students. What is the difference in the two words: student and students?* Explain that the letter *s* is often added to the end of a word to show that there is more than one.

USING PAGE 16

Ask students to:
- point to letter *e* that stands for /e/
- listen as you read words in box
- locate words as you repeat them
- read aloud and track words with you

Point to the pen in the top box. *Is there one pen or more than one pen?* Have the students look at the second illustration. Read *lots of pens* aloud to the class and ask the students to repeat it. *Is there one pen or more than one pen?* Point out that one pen is described as *a* pen, but the word *a* does not appear before more than one pen or *pens.* Review the pairs of singular and plural words in the box, pointing out the *a* before the singular words and the plural *s.*

INCLUDING ALL LEARNERS

Ring the Bell or Bells!
(Auditory Learners)

Materials: assorted groups of items, such as bells, mitts, hats, and pens

Hold up an item (a bell, for example), and say, *I have one bell.* Ring the bell. Then hold up two bells and say, *I have two bells.* Ring the two bells. Hand a bell to a student who will say, *I have one bell.* Then

he or she can ring the bell. Repeat with more than one bell. Continue this oral activity using different objects until all the students have had a turn.

Say It!

Recite simple sentences containing either singular or plural forms of words students have used in the exercise on this page, such as *a pen, pens, a cat, cats, a mitt, mitts.* Ask students to raise one hand if they hear the singular word and two hands if they hear the plural word. Then ask students to make sentences with singular and plural forms of the words and recite them. ✓

Write It!

Draw or display pictures of one hat, two hats, one bag, and two bags. Ask the students to write the word for each picture, including the final *s* if the picture shows more than one of an item. When they are finished, review the work as a class or in small groups. ✓

Little Book: *The Bus*

Key Words: bus, get, Gus

Phonics Objectives

Can students:
✓ listen for the short vowel sounds /a/, /o/, /i/, /u/, and /e/?
✓ read letters for short vowels in words in the context of a story?
✓ write words with short vowels?

Language Acquisition Objectives

Can students:
✓ read words in story context?
✓ use the verbs *is, is not, can, cannot*?

ESL Standards

• Goal 1, Standard 2

DEVELOPING PHONEMIC AWARENESS

Invite students to listen as you recite (or play) the chant below. Say the word *hops* and model oral blending: *hooooopsss.* Ask them to listen for all the short vowel sounds /o/, /u/, and /e/.

> Gus, Gus
> Hops on the bus, bus.
> Gus, Gus
> Hops on the bus, bus.
> Gus, Gus,
> Get off the bus, Gus!
> Gus, Gus,
> Get off the bus!

Invite children to recite the chant with you and then as a group on their own. Let them pretend to tell Gus to get off the bus in the second half of the chant by cupping their hands by the sides of their mouth as if shouting or by motioning.

USING THE LITTLE BOOK

Explain to the students that they are going to make a Little Book about Gus the dog. Ask them to remove pages 17 and 18 from their books. Show them how to cut the page on the dotted line with the scissors icon, then fold the pages to make their own eight-page Little Book.

Preview *The Bus* by reading the title aloud. Allow the students time to look through the book and examine the pictures. Ask the students to follow along and track the words in the Little Book as you read the story aloud to them.

Engage the class in the story. Draw upon the students' experiences and feelings about the story to spark their interest. Ask them questions such as *Do you ride a bus to school or to get places? Do you ever see an animal on a bus?*

Revisit the story. Lead the class in a second reading of *The Bus.* This time, ask for volunteers to read aloud one page at a time. After each page is read, ask questions focusing on the content of the story. Here are some examples:

• *Who is on the bus?*
• *Who cannot get on the bus?*
• *What do children say to Gus?*

INCLUDING ALL LEARNERS

Act Out the Story: *The Bus*
(Kinesthetic/Auditory Learners)

Arrange pairs of chairs as if they were seats on a bus. Place a single seat in front to serve as the driver's seat. Ask for five volunteers to act out the story *The Bus*. Assign the roles of Bob, Nan, Tim, Gus the dog, and the bus driver.

Have the volunteers act out the story as you read it aloud to the class. Remind them to say "Get off the bus, Gus! Gus! Get off the bus!" after you read the sentence *Gus hops on the bus*. (Rehearse this if necessary.)

When you are done, call on a new group of actors. Ask a volunteer to read the story aloud while the actors perform it. Encourage other groups of students to perform the story for the class.

Story Time
(Extra Help)

Give students time to read the story quietly. Have students give summaries of what happens in the story. Then encourage students to tell their own pet or animal stories. They can tell true stories or far-fetched adventure stories. Have students get into small groups and tell their stories.

Say It!

 To help your students remember the short vowel sounds, you can teach them the following chant.

> Did you learn short *i*?
> I did, did, did!
> Did you learn short *e*?
> Oh, yes, yes, yes!
> Can you say short *a*?
> I can, can, can!
> Do you like short *o*?
> It's top, top, tops!
> Do you like short *u*?
> Very much, much, much!

You probably will want to teach them the chant one pair of lines at a time. ✓

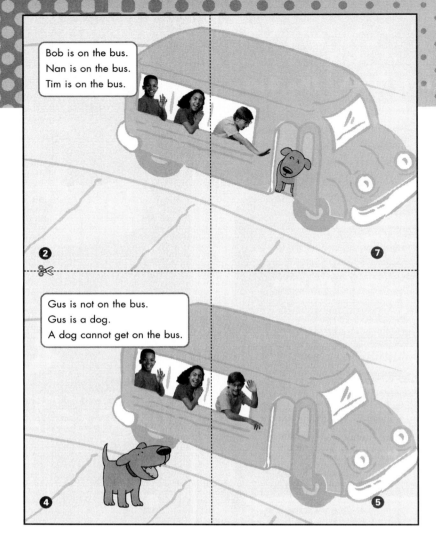

Bob is on the bus.
Nan is on the bus.
Tim is on the bus.

❷ ❼

Gus is not on the bus.
Gus is a dog.
A dog cannot get on the bus.

❹ ❺

Write It!

Write the following sentences on the chalkboard. Ask the students to copy them, filling in the blanks with the correct word or words.

- Gus _____ a dog. (<u>is</u>, is not)
- Bob, Nan, and Tim _____ get on the bus. (<u>can</u>, cannot)
- Tim _____ a dog. (is, <u>is not</u>)
- Gus _____ get on the bus. (can, <u>cannot</u>)
- Gus _____ sad. (<u>is</u>, is not)

When they are finished, review the activity as a class. ✓

Family Connection

 Send home the Little Book *The Bus*. Encourage students to read the book to a family member.

BOOK CORNER

/e/ e
Clifford Gets a Job
by Norman Bridwell

/e/ e
The Little Red Hen
by Paul Galdone

/u/ u
The Ugly Duckling
by Hans Christian Andersen

/u/ u
Clifford at the Circus
by Norman Bridwell

/e/ e, /u/ u
Peanuts comic strips
by Charles Schultz

/e/ e, /u/ u
The Wheels on the Bus
by Maryann Kovalski

Short Vowels

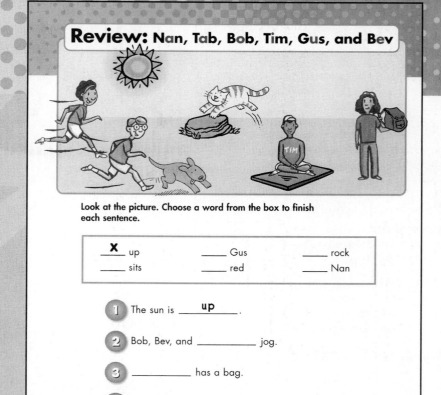

Review: Nan, Tab, Bob, Tim, Gus, and Bev

Look at the picture. Choose a word from the box to finish each sentence.

x up	_____ Gus	_____ rock
_____ sits	_____ red	_____ Nan

1 The sun is ____**up**____.

2 Bob, Bev, and _____ jog.

3 _____ has a bag.

4 Nan's bag is _____.

5 Tab hops on a _____.

6 Tim _____ on a mat.

Phonics Objectives

Can students:

✓ listen for and identify the short vowel sounds /a/, /o/, /i/, /u/, and /e/?

✓ read and write letters for short vowels *a, o, i, u,* and *e* in words and sentences?

Language Acquisition Objectives

Students:

• review verbs
• use words relating to the outdoors

ESL Standards

• Goal 2, Standard 1

DEVELOPING PHONEMIC AWARENESS

Congratulate your class for learning all of the short vowel sounds. Place two chairs at the front of the class and ask for two volunteers to sit in them. Hand one student a card with the letter *u* on it and the other student a card with the letter *e* on it. Tell them to listen as you say a list of words. If they hear a word with the short vowel sound for their letter, they should *pop up.* Use the following words: *bed, red, rug, hug, pen, nut, fun, pets, bug, sun.* You may wish to say the words as you model oral blending first. For example, say the word *rug: rrrruuuuug.*

Continue the activity with other students, replacing *u* and *e* with short vowel letters *a, o, i,* and words with the corresponding short vowel sounds. Make the activity more difficult by adding words that do not have the sounds.

USING THE REVIEW PAGE

Ask students to:

• point to the letters *a, o, i, u, e*
• listen as you read words in box
• locate words as you repeat them
• read aloud and track words with you

Ask the class to look at the title of the page. Read the name *Nan* aloud. Ask students what other short *a* words they know. Continue with the other names in the title, reviewing short vowel words.

Ask students to examine the outdoor scene and talk about what each Phonics Team character is doing. Invite them to talk about different things they do outdoors.

INCLUDING ALL LEARNERS

Listen for Sounds!
(Kinesthetic/Auditory Learners)

Play a game similar to Musical Chairs with your students, but instead of listening to music, they will listen to words. When they hear a word with a short vowel sound, they should stop circling the chairs and try to find a seat. The student left standing is out of the game. (Also, if a student sits after a word that does not have the short vowel sound, he or she is out of the game.) Remove one chair and continue the game until only one student is seated.

Say It!

Let students work in pairs to create sentences with a word with a short vowel sound. One partner recites his or her sentence and the listening partner identifies the word(s) with the short vowel sound. Then partners switch so the listening partner recites a sentence. ✓

Write It!

Ask students to write the following words each on a separate line: *Nan, Tab, Bob, Tim, Gus,* and *Bev.* Next to each word, have students add words they know that have the same short vowel sound. ✓

UNIT 3

Blends

Initial *l*-Blends: *cl, fl, pl, bl, gl, sl*

Key Words: o'clock, flag, plant, black, glass, sled

Phonics Objectives

Can students:
- ✓ listen for the sounds of initial *l*-blends *cl, fl, pl, bl, gl,* and *sl*?
- ✓ identify the sounds the letter combinations *cl, fl, pl, bl, gl,* and *sl* stand for?
- ✓ read and write initial *l*-blends in words and sentences?

Language Acquisition Objectives

Students:
- use words relating to the classroom

ESL Standards
- Goal 2, Standard 1

DEVELOPING PHONEMIC AWARENESS

Pronounce the word *cap* for the class, stressing the /k/ sound. Next, say the word *lap*, stressing the /l/ sound. Say the word *clap* and model oral blending: *cllllaaaaap*. Pronounce the word *clap* more quickly and clap your hands. Ask students to do the same. Point out how the *cl* combines the sounds /k/ and /l/.

Challenge the class to listen carefully as you say a list of words. If a word begins with the same sound as *clap*, they should clap their hands. You may wish to use the following list of words: *cat, class, club, lab, can, cub, club*. You can repeat this activity with initial *l*-blends *fl, pl, bl, gl,* and *sl*.

USING THE PAGES

Page 20

Ask students to:
- point to the letters *cl, fl, pl, bl, gl, sl*
- locate words as you say them
- read aloud and track words with you

Read the title "In the Class" aloud and explain that in this lesson students will learn names for things that can be found in the classroom. Say the word *class*, stressing the initial *cl*. Have the class repeat the word after you. Then use the other words and illustrations in the box to point out the sound of *cl* as in *o'clock, fl* as in *flag, pl* as in *plant, bl* as in *black, gl* as in *glass,* and *sl* as in *sled*.

Point out the word *o'clock* in the box. Explain that when a number word comes before *o'clock*, this tells the exact hour on the clock.

Page 21

Invite students to look over the large illustration at the top of the page. Ask a volunteer to read aloud the sentence that is written on the blackboard in the picture. *(Gus is in the class.)*

Write *cl, fl, pl, bl, gl,* and *sl* on the chalkboard. Direct students' attention to the objects in the illustration which have names that begin with the letter combinations you have written. Point to each blend as you say the word. *(class, clock, blackboard, flag, plant)* Challenge students to find things in the classroom that begin with any of these blends.

Gus is in the class.

Circle *yes* if the sentence matches the picture.
Circle *no* if it does not.

1. Gus is in the class.   (yes)   no
2. A bus is in the class.   yes   no
3. Gus has Nan's bag.   yes   no
4. The bag is black.   yes   no
5. Gus is on a sled.   yes   no
6. A bell is in the class.   yes   no
7. Gus has a glass.   yes   no
8. Gus is a black dog.   yes   no
9. A flag is in the class.   yes   no
10. It is ten o'clock.   yes   no

Initial Blends: *cl, fl, pl, bl, gl, sl*   **Unit 3 21**

Say It!

 Teach the class the following chant.

> At one o'clock, wave the flag.
> At two o'clock, fill the bag.
> At three o'clock, go to class.
> At four o'clock, ride the sled.

Call on students to identify and say the words with the initial *fl, cl,* and *sl* sounds. Ask volunteers to model blending the sounds in the words. After the class recites the chant, you can extend the activity by helping students create additional lines that include words with these sounds. ✔

Write It!

 Distribute writing paper to each student. One at a time, display magazine cutout pictures for the initial *l*-blend words. Ask students to say the word for each picture and write the first two letters. Review the work as a class. ✔

INCLUDING ALL LEARNERS

Set the Clock!
(Kinesthetic Learners)

Materials: a time-teaching clock or any clock whose hands can be moved manually

Ask the class to stand. Set the clock for twelve and say, *It's twelve o'clock.* Invite students to stick up their arms as if they were a clock at twelve o'clock. Have them repeat *It's twelve o'clock* after you. Move the clock to one o'clock and repeat the activity. Continue in this manner until students have positioned their arms and said the hour for all the hours on a clock.

Make Flags
(Visual Learners)

Materials: construction paper, glue, tape or stapler, string, scissors, markers

On the chalkboard, write the initial *l*-blend words *clock, flag, plant, black, glass,* and *sled.* Distribute the construction paper, glue, scissors, and markers. Ask students to draw a picture of their country's flag. Then ask them to cut the construction paper into the shape of a flag.

Place a long piece of string along a bulletin board or wall. Have each student present his or her flag and name the picture on it. Then tape or staple the flag to the string.

Match the Sounds!
(Extra Help)

Materials: index cards, markers

On large index cards, write the words *clock, flag, plant, glass,* and *sled.* Say each word aloud as you display it on the chalk rail. Invite the class to repeat it after you.

Next, say the word *plug* and ask a volunteer to lift up the index card that has the word that begins with the same sound *(plant).* Repeat this activity with other words beginning with *cl, fl, pl, gl,* and *sl.* Some words you may use are *flop, clap, glad, slap, slip, flat,* and *plum.*

Initial *r*-Blends: *gr, fr, br, tr, cr, dr*

Key Words: grass, frog, brick, truck, crab, dress

Phonics Objectives

Can students:
- ✓ listen for the sounds of initial *r*-blends *gr, fr, br, tr, cr,* and *dr*?
- ✓ identify the sounds the letter combinations *gr, fr, br, tr, cr,* and *dr* stand for?
- ✓ read and write initial *r*-blends in words and sentences?

Language Acquisition Objectives

Students:
- use words relating to the outdoors

ESL Standards
- Goal 1, Standard 1

On the Grass

grass   frog   brick   truck   crab   dress

Match the sentences with the pictures.

1. The frog is on the grass.
2. The crab is not on the grass.
3. Bev has a red dress.
4. Bob drops a red brick.
5. Gus is in the truck.

a
b
c
d
e

22 Unit 3
Initial Blends: *gr, fr, br, tr, cr, dr;* Verb: *drop*

DEVELOPING PHONEMIC AWARENESS

Pronounce the word *rap* for the class, stressing the /r/ sound. Next, do the same for the word *tap*, stressing the /t/ sound. Say the word *trap* and model oral blending: *trrrraaaaap.* Then pronounce the word *trap* and ask the students to repeat it after you. (If necessary, define the word for the class.) Point out how the initial *tr* combines the /t/ and /r/ sounds.

Challenge the class to listen carefully as you say a list of words. If a word begins with the same sound as *trap*, they should tap their foot three times. You may wish to use the following list of words: *top, trot, track, tick, trick, trust, tuck, truck.* You can repeat this activity with initial *r*-blends *gr, fr, br, cr,* and *dr.*

USING PAGE 22

Ask students to:
- point to the letters *gr, fr, br, tr, cr, dr*
- locate words as you say them
- read aloud and track words with you

Point out the picture of grass in the box. Show students how in the word *grass* the /g/ and /r/ sounds combine. Use the other words and illustrations in the box to introduce the initial *fr* as in *frog, br* as in *brick, tr* as in *truck, cr* as in *crab,* and *dr* as in *dress.*

INCLUDING ALL LEARNERS

What's on the Grass?
(Visual Learners)

Materials: drawing paper, markers

Distribute the drawing materials, and ask students to draw a picture of something that might be on the grass outside. Work as a class to decorate a bulletin board with green grass and their finished pictures of outdoor things.

Say It!

 Teach the class the following chant. 🎧

There's a frog in a dress.
A dr . . . dr . . . dress!
There's a dog on a brick.
A br . . . br . . . brick!
There's a crab in a truck.
A tr . . . tr . . . truck!
Can this be, be, be
A tr . . . tr . . . trick?

Call on students to identify and say the words with the initial *fr, dr, cr, tr,* and *br* sounds. Extend the activity by letting students vary the chant by rearranging the sentences. (Example: *There's a crab in a dress.*) ✓

Write It!

Distribute writing paper to each student. One at a time, display magazine cutout pictures for the initial *r*-blend words. Ask students to say the word for each picture and write the first two letters. ✓

Initial s-Blends: *st, sp, sn, sw, sk, sm*

Key Words: step, spill, snack, swim, skip, smell

Phonics Objectives

Can students:
- ✓ listen for sounds of initial *s*-blends *st, sp, sn, sw, sk,* and *sm?*
- ✓ identify the sounds the letter combinations *st, sp, sn, sw, sk,* and *sm* stand for?
- ✓ read and write initial *s*-blends in words and sentences?

Language Acquisition Objectives

Can students:
- ✓ use the verbs *spill, swim, skip, smell?*

ESL Standards

- Goal 1, Standard 2

On the Steps

steps   spill   snack   swim   Bev skips.   smell

Match the sentences with the pictures.

1. A big stick is on the steps.
2. Bev skips.
3. The snack spills.
4. Nan can smell the snack.
5. Tim can swim.

a
b
c
d
e

Initial Blends: *st, sp, sn, sw, sk, sm;* Verbs: *spill, swim, skip, smell*

Unit 3 23

DEVELOPING PHONEMIC AWARENESS

Say the word *sand,* stressing the initial /s/ sound. Next, say the word *nap,* stressing the /n/ sound. Say the word *snap* and model oral blending: *snnnnaaaaap.* Then, pronounce the word *snap* as you snap your fingers. Invite students to say the word and snap their fingers. Point out how the *sn* combines the /s/ and /n/ sounds.

Challenge the class to listen carefully as you say a list of words. If a word begins with the same sound as *snap,* they should snap their fingers. You may wish to use the following list of words: *snip, sip, snug, some, snooze, sat, snack.* You can repeat this activity with initial *s*-blends *st, sp, sw, sk,* and *sm.*

USING PAGE 23

Ask students to:
- point to the letters *st, sn, sw, sk, sm*
- locate words as you say them
- read aloud and track words with you

Point to the picture of the steps on the page and say the word *steps,* stressing the initial *st.* Point out how the /s/ and /t/ sounds combine. Have the class repeat it. Use the other words and illustrations in the box to introduce the initial *sp* as in *spill, sn* as in *snack, sw* as in *swim, sk* as in *skips,* and *sm* as in *smell.*

INCLUDING ALL LEARNERS

Skip to My Lou
(Auditory Learners)

Teach the class the song "Skip to My Lou." Once they learn the song, invite them to skip as they sing it. 🎧

Skip, skip, skip to my Lou.
Skip, skip, skip to my Lou.
Skip, skip, skip to my Lou.
Skip to my Lou, my darling!

Say It!

Play a charades game by writing the words *step, swim, skip, smell,* and *snack* on slips of paper and placing them in a hat. Divide the class into teams and invite members of each team to act out a word that they pick from the hat for their team. Give points to teams that guess the right word. ✔

Write It!

Ask students to listen carefully as you read a list of words. Instruct them to write down the first two letters of each word they hear. Use the following words, stressing the sounds of the initial *s*-blends: *snack, spill, step, swim, smell,* and *skip.* ✔

Final Blends: *nd, lk, mp, nk, ft*

Key Words: sand, milk, jump, tank, gift

Phonics Objectives

Can students:
- ✔ listen for the sounds of final blends *nd, lk, mp, nk,* and *ft?*
- ✔ identify the sounds the letter combinations *nd, lk, mp, nk,* and *ft* stand for?
- ✔ read and write words and sentences containing final blends *nd, lk, mp, nk,* and *ft?*

Language Acquisition Objectives

Can students:
- ✔ use verbs?

ESL Standards

- Goal 1, Standard 1

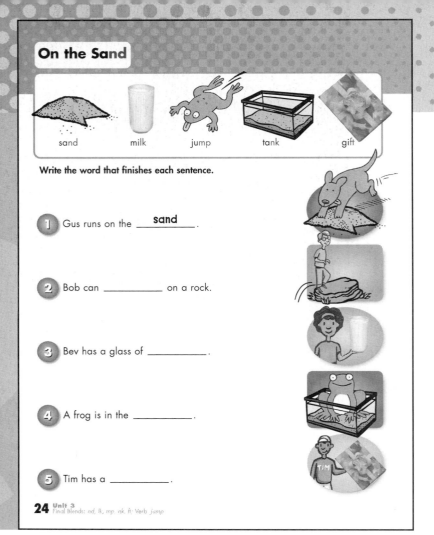

On the Sand

sand   milk   jump   tank   gift

Write the word that finishes each sentence.

1. Gus runs on the ___**sand**___.

2. Bob can _____ on a rock.

3. Bev has a glass of _____.

4. A frog is in the _____.

5. Tim has a _____.

24 Unit 3
Final Blends: *nd, lk, mp, nk, ft;* Verb *jump*

DEVELOPING PHONEMIC AWARENESS

Pronounce the word *bed* for the class, stressing the final /d/ sound. Next, say the name *Ben*, stressing the /n/ sound. Say the word *bend* and model oral blending: *beeeennnnd.* Then pronounce the word *bend,* as you bend your body. Point out how the final *nd* combines the sounds the letters *n* and *d* stand for. Have the students make the sound of *nd* with you.

Introduce the word *hand* as you show your *hand.* Point out that *hand* has the same final sound as *bend.* Ask the class to listen as you say a list of words. If a word ends with the same sound as *hand,* students should raise their hands as they repeat the word. You may wish to use the following list of words: _band_, *bug,* _bin_, _sand_, *sat, snack,* _land_. You can repeat this activity with final blends *lk, mp, nk,* and *ft.*

USING PAGE 24

Ask students to:
- point to letters *nd, lk, mp, nk, ft*
- locate words as you say them
- read aloud and track words with you

Point out the picture of the sand in the box. Explain how in the word *sand* the /n/ and the /d/ combine to make the *nd.* Invite the class to make the sound of *nd.* Use the other words and illustrations in the box to introduce the final *lk* as in *milk, mp* as in *jump, nk* as in *tank,* and *ft* as in *gift.*

INCLUDING ALL LEARNERS

Final Blend Concentration
(Kinesthetic/Visual Learners)

Materials: index cards

Students will form words by matching the beginnings of words with their final blend endings in this game. Use the following words: *sand, milk, jump, tank, gift.* Write

the first two letters of each word on one card and the last two letters on another. Mix up the cards and place them face-down. Write the words on the chalkboard, then invite two students to play the game. The first player turns over two cards. If they form one of the words on the chalk-board, the student must say the word. If correct, he or she can keep the cards.

Say It!

Play "Simon Says" with the students. If they hear the action word with a final blend in the direction, they should say the word and do the action. If not, they should stay still. You can use directions like these: *Simon says jump. Simon says stand. Simon says lift your leg.* ✔

Write It!

Ask the students to listen carefully as you read a list of words. Instruct them to write down the last two letters of each word they hear. Use the following words, stressing the final blend: *tank, jump, milk, sand,* and *gift.* ✔

Final Blends: *xt, st, sk, lp, lt, nt*

Key Words: next, nest, desk, help, belt, tent

Next to Bev

Bob is next to Bev. nest · desk · Help! · belt · tent

Write the word that finishes each sentence.

1. The frog is ____next____ to the rock.

2. The belt is on Nan's _____.

3. Gus is next to the _____.

4. The frog is in a _____.

5. Tim yells, "_____!"

Help!

Final Blends: *xt, st, sk, lp, lt, nt;* Prepositions: *next to, in, on* **25**

DEVELOPING PHONEMIC AWARENESS

Make the /s/ sound. Have the class repeat it. Say the /k/ sound, having the class repeat it. Then point to a desk and say *desk,* focusing on the final *sk.* Say the word *desk* and model oral blending: *deeeessssk.* Invite the class to repeat it after you. Repeat this with the sounds in the other final blends *xt* as in *next, st* as in *first, lp* as in *help,* and *lt* as in *belt.*

USING PAGE 25

Ask students to:
- point to the letters *xt, st, sk, lp, lt, nt*
- locate words as you say them
- read aloud and track words with you

Point out the picture of Bob standing next to Bev in the box. Read *Bob is next to Bev* aloud. Point out how in the word *next,* the *x* and the *t* together stand for the /kst/ sound. Ask a student in the front row to

say the word *next,* and then ask the student behind him or her to say it. Continue until all the students have said *next.* Use the other words and illustrations in the box to introduce the final *st* as in *nest, sk* as in *desk, lp* as in *help, lt* as in *belt,* and *nt* as in *tent.*

INCLUDING ALL LEARNERS

The Nest
(Auditory Learners)

Teach your class the following rhyme. Help them identify the final blends in the words *next, tent, nest, sing, rest.*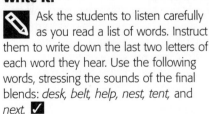

> Next to my tent
> I hear birds in a nest.
> The birds sing and sing
> So I get no rest!

Say It!

Ask the students to line up in a row. Stand on the left end of the row and say, *I am next to (name of student*

on your right). Then ask that student to say, *I am next to (name of student on his or her right).* Have students continue down the line. When they reach the end, ask the student on the far right to reverse the process, naming the student on his or her left. ✓

Write It!

Ask the students to listen carefully as you read a list of words. Instruct them to write down the last two letters of each word they hear. Use the following words, stressing the sounds of the final blends: *desk, belt, help, nest, tent,* and *next.* ✓

Initial /kw/ *qu*

Key Words: quack, quiz

Quack Quiz

quack, quack

THE POND

Circle *yes* if the sentence matches the picture.
Circle *no* if it does not.

1. Gus and Bev swim in the pond.   yes   (no)
2. A frog is not on the rock; it is gone.   yes   no
3. Tab is on a desk.   yes   no
4. Ducks swim in the pond.   yes   no
5. A flag is on the rock.   yes   no
6. Nan's belt is on the sand.   yes   no
7. Ducks can quack.   yes   no
8. Tab can quack.   yes   no
9. A crab is in the pond.   yes   no
10. The pond has grass in it.   yes   no

26 Unit 3
/Kw/ qu and Blends

Phonics Objectives

Can students:
✓ listen for /kw/ *qu*?
✓ identify the sound the letter combination *qu* stands for?
✓ read and write the letter combination *qu* in words and sentences?

Language Acquisition Objectives

Can students:
✓ use the prepositions *in* and *on*?

ESL Standards

• Goal 2, Standard 1

DEVELOPING PHONEMIC AWARENESS

Pronounce the word *quack* for the class, stressing the *qu* sound. Ask students to repeat the word after you. Ask students what sound they hear at the beginning of the word: /kw/. Let them repeat the sound and ask them which animal makes that sound. Challenge volunteers to model blending the sounds in the word *quack*. Point out how the sound is made up of /k/ and /w/ sounds that form the new /kw/ sound.

Play a game in which students say *quack* when they hear a word that begins with /kw/. Use the following words: *quick, quit, can, quilt, cream,* and *guava.*

USING PAGE 26

Read the title "Quack Quiz" aloud. Explain that *quack* is the sound that a duck makes and that *quiz* is another word for *test.*

Ask a volunteer to say what the ducks in the picture are saying. Ask another student to read what is on the sign. Challenge the students to name other parts of the picture that they recognize.

INCLUDING ALL LEARNERS

Quiet Things
(Visual Learners)

Materials: drawing paper, crayons or markers

Write the word *quiet* on the blackboard and pronounce it. Brainstorm things and places that are *quiet*. Distribute the drawing materials and ask the students to draw quiet things. Create a bulletin board titled "Quiet Things" using the students' finished drawings.

Say It!

 Teach the class the following rhyme. 🎧

   I have a duck
   That brings me lunch.

   Quack, quack (clap, clap)
   Quack, quack (clap, clap)

   He's green and black
   With a shiny back.
   Quack, quack (clap, clap)
   Quack, quack (clap, clap)

Ask students to clap whenever they hear the word with the initial /kw/ sound. Divide the class into two groups and have them recite the rhyme as a round. ✔

Write It!

✏ Write the following sentences on the chalkboard. Ask students to write down only the sentences that are true.

   A book is in the class.
   A duck is on the desk.
   A shoe is on my foot.
   A bug is in my hat.

You can extend this activity by asking each student to write a true/false quiz for a friend. ✔

Little Book: *The Frog*

Key Words: frog, glass, tank, desk, class, plant, sand, grass, black, swim, pond, clock, flag, jump, land, snack, spill, milk, next, help, step

Phonics Objectives

Can students:
- ✓ listen for the sounds of initial and final blends?
- ✓ read initial and final blends in the context of a story?
- ✓ write words with initial and final blends?

Language Acquisition Objectives

Can students:
- ✓ read words in story context?
- ✓ use the prepositions *in, on*?

ESL Standards
- Goal 1, Standard 2

DEVELOPING PHONEMIC AWARENESS

Invite students to listen as you recite (or play) the chant below. Ask them to listen for all the blend sounds.

> The frog's in the class.
> The frog's in the grass.
> It lands on the pond.
> It swims to the land.
> Hop, frog, hop!

Choose words from the chant to model oral blending. For example, say the word *lands: lllllaaaaannnndsss.* Invite students to recite the chant with you and then as a group on their own.

USING THE LITTLE BOOK

Tell the students that they can make a Little Book about a frog. Ask them to remove pages 27 and 28 from their books. Show them how to cut the page on the dotted line with the scissors icon, then fold the pages to make their own eight-page Little Book.

Preview *The Frog* by reading the title aloud. Allow the students time to look through the book and examine the pictures. Ask the students to follow along as you read the story aloud to them.

Engage the class in the story. You can prompt the discussion by asking questions that bring in their own personal experiences and opinions, such as *Have you ever seen a frog? What do you know about frogs? If there was a frog in this classroom, what would you do?*

Revisit the book. Lead the class in a second reading of *The Frog*. This time, invite volunteers to read aloud one page at a time. After each page is read, ask questions focusing on the content of the story. Here are some examples:

- *Where does the story take place?*
- *What does the frog do?*
- *Where does the frog go? Why?*

INCLUDING ALL LEARNERS

Hop, Frog, Hop!
(Kinesthetic Learners)

Materials: markers or crayons, construction paper, scissors, pipe cleaners, pictures of frogs

Tell the class that they are going to make their own frogs. Distribute materials. Display pictures of frogs for the students to examine, then ask them to draw and decorate a frog of their own. Instruct them to cut out their frog when they are finished. They can attach pipe cleaners or fold strips of paper accordian-style to make frog legs.

On the chalkboard, write *on, in,* and *next to.* Borrow a student's frog and put it on top of a book. Say, *The frog is on the book.* Ask the class to repeat the sentence. Then, put the frog next to something in the class and say, *The frog is next to the _____.* Ask the class to repeat it after you. Ask a volunteer to take her or his frog and place it *in, on,* and *next to* objects in the room. Have the student say the appropriate sentences. *(The frog is in . . .)* One at a time, have other students do the same. Continue until everyone has had a turn at least once.

Where's the Frog?
(Extra Help)

Read the story aloud to the class again, but pause after each page to ask questions to check your students' comprehension. Here are some suggestions:

Page 2:
• *What is on the desk? (a tank)*
• *What is in the tank? (a plant, sand, grass, pond, a frog)*

Page 4:
• *Why isn't the frog in the tank anymore? (He jumped out.)*
• *Where was the frog hiding? (behind the flag)*

Page 6:
• *What does Nan yell? (Help! Get the frog! It is on the steps!)*
• *Do they catch the frog? (no)*
• *Where does the frog go? (outside)*

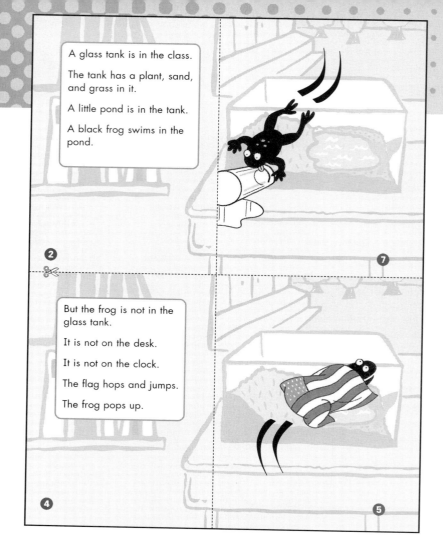

A glass tank is in the class.

The tank has a plant, sand, and grass in it.

A little pond is in the tank.

A black frog swims in the pond.

But the frog is not in the glass tank.

It is not on the desk.

It is not on the clock.

The flag hops and jumps.

The frog pops up.

Say It!

 Give students time to read the story aloud. Then engage the class in a discussion about words they read in the story. *What letter sounds do you know in the words? Which words have blends in them?* ✓

Write It!

Instruct your class to listen carefully as you ask them some questions about the story. Tell them that they may look through their Little Books before they write down their answers.

1. Who is the story about? *(a frog)*
2. On pages 2 and 3, where is the frog? *(in the pond, in the tank)*
3. On pages 4 and 5, was the frog on the clock? *(no)*
4. On pages 6 and 7, what does the frog do to Nan's snack? *(spills it)*
5. On page 8, where does the frog go? *(outside, on the steps)* ✓

Family Connection

Send the Little Book *The Frog* home with the students. Encourage them to read the book to a family member.

BOOK CORNER

/kl/ cl *Clocks and More Clocks* by Pat Hutchins

/fr/ fr, /pr/ pr
The Frog Prince by Edith H. Tarcov

/lk/ lk *Jack and the Beanstalk* by Matt Faulkner

/sm/ sm *Fireman Small* by Wong Herbert Yee

/kst/ xt *The Bear Next* by Ida Luttrell

/kw/ qu, /kr/ cr
The Very Quiet Cricket by Eric Carle

Blends and Short Vowels

Phonics Objectives

Can students:
- ✓ listen for and identify sounds of initial and final blends?
- ✓ Read and write words and sentences with short vowels and initial and final blends?

Language Acquisition Objectives

Can students:
- ✓ use verbs?

ESL Standards

- Goal 2, Standard 1

Review: Blends and Short Vowels

cat	grass	bus	pens	hit
desk	dog	jump	dress	sits

Self Test: Write the word that finishes each sentence.

1. Tab is a fat ____cat____ .

2. Gus is a big _____ .

3. Tim can _____ the ball.

4. Gus and Bob can _____ .

5. Nan and Bob get on the _____ .

6. Bev has ten red _____ .

7. A frog is in the _____ .

8. A plant is on the _____ .

9. Tim _____ on a hill.

10. Bev has a red _____ .

Review of Blends, Short Vowels, and Verbs **Unit 3 29**

DEVELOPING PHONEMIC AWARENESS

To practice the initial and final blends introduced in Unit 3, ask students to repeat a series of action words using those blends. As they repeat each word after you, invite the class to mime the action suggested by the word. If students have difficulty, you can mime the action yourself and have them copy you. Use the following words: *jump, grab, swing, clap, flap, climb, step, swim, smell, skip.*

USING THE REVIEW PAGE

Ask students to:
- point to the letters *sk, gr, mp, dr*
- locate words as you say them
- read aloud and track words with you

Ask the class to look at the words in the box at the top of the page. Ask for volun-teers to read each word aloud. You may want to point out the words that contain blends: *grass, desk, jump,* and *dress.* Tell the class that they are going to use those words to complete sentences on the page.

INCLUDING ALL LEARNERS

Make a Blend Clock
(Visual Learners)

Materials: newspapers and magazines, scissors, construction paper, tacks or sta-ples, markers

Divide the class into twelve pairs or groups. Distribute the magazines and newspapers and ask each group to look for pictures of or draw things whose names have the blends taught in this unit. When the groups have their pictures, work as a class to make a clock on the bulletin board. At each hour on the clock, tack one of the pictures representing a blend word.

Say It!

Shuffle index cards with the words *jump, hit, sit, grab, stomp, stop, clap, skip, spill,* and *smell* written on them. Then ask a volunteer to come to the front of the class. Ask the student to read a card without showing it to the other stu-dents. Ask him or her to act out the action written on the card, and challenge the other students to guess and say the word that is written on the card. The student who first guesses correctly gets to pick the next card and act out the word. ✓

Write It!

Distribute writing paper to each student. One at a time, display magazine cutout pictures for the initial and final blends covered in Unit 3. Ask the stu-dents to write the word for each picture and circle the first or last two letters. ✓

UNIT 4

Long Vowels: a

Long Vowels: /ā/ a-e

Key Words: Kate, make, cake, take, plate, wake, wave, lake, snake

Phonics Objectives

Can students:
- ✓ listen for the long *a* sound?
- ✓ identify the long *a* sound formed by the letter combination *a-e*?
- ✓ read and write words and sentences with the long *a (a-e)* sound?

Language Acquisition Objectives

Students:
- use the verbs *make, take, wake.*

ESL Standards

- Goal 2, Standard 2

UNIT 4 Long Vowels: a | a-e | Kate makes a cake.

Kate takes a plate.

Kate makes a cake.

waves in a lake

Kate wakes up.

snake

Match the sentences with the pictures.

1. Kate makes a sand cake.
2. Kate wakes up at six o'clock.
3. Kate's plate has grapes on it.
4. The lake has waves.
5. The snake is not in the lake.

a
b
c
d
e

30 Unit 4
Long Vowels /ā/a-e; Verbs *make, take, wake*

DEVELOPING PHONEMIC AWARENESS

Say the word *cap.* Ask a student to repeat the word. Explain that this word has a short *a* sound. Then tell the class when you add the letter *e* to the end of *cap* it becomes the new word *cape.* Say the word *cape* and model oral blending: *caaaaape.* Let the class repeat it. Explain that this word has the long *a* sound.

Say the word *wave,* model oral blending, and then ask the class to repeat the word and wave their hands. Ask if *wave* has the long *a* sound. *(yes)* Tell students to listen carefully as you say some words. Ask them to repeat each word and, if it has the long *a* sound, wave their hands over their heads. You can use the following words: *pig, place, cat, cake, cave, bug, lake, hop.*

USING PAGE 30

Ask students to:
- point to the letters *a-e*
- locate words as you say them
- read aloud and track words with you

Read aloud the sentence *Kate makes a cake.* Ask volunteers to tell you the letter that falls between the *a* and the *e* in Kate. Do the same with *make* and *cake.* Write *Kate, makes,* and *cake* on the chalkboard. Point out the vowel-consonant-vowel (vcv) pattern in each word and explain that *a-e* stands for the long *a* sound.

INCLUDING ALL LEARNERS

Make a Long-*a* Plate!
(Visual Learners)

Materials: white paper plates, markers

Hold up a paper plate. Write *plate* on the chalkboard and point out the long *a* sound. Then distribute materials. Ask students to draw a picture of a long *a* word.

Say It!

 Teach students the following chant.

> Look out, Kate!
> There's a crab on your plate!
> I think that
> he wants to eat your cake.
> Take that crab
> and throw him in the lake!

Teach the chant as a group, then invite students to recite it to the class. ✓

Write It!

Write the words *lake, snake, plate, cake,* and *wake* on the chalkboard. Then read the following riddles to the class. After each riddle, have students write down the long *a* word answer.

You can put food on me. *(plate)*
You do this every morning. *(wake)*
You can swim in me. *(lake)*
I'm an animal with no legs. *(snake)*
You get this on your birthday. *(cake)*

Long Vowels: /ā/ ay

Key Words: play, gray, day, say, lay, crayon

ay | **Kate plays.**

Bob and Nan say, "Hey, Kate!"

Hey, Kate!

Kate plays on a gray day.

Kate lays a crayon on the desk.

Write the word to match the picture.

1. Kate and Tab ___**play**___ .
   say/play

2. The crayon is _____ .
   gray/red

3. Kate lays a _____ of grapes on the desk.
   plate/snake

4. Bob and Nan _____ , "Hey!"
   play/say

5. Kate _____ up at ten o'clock.
   waves/wakes

Long Vowels /ā/ay; Verbs: play, say, lay **31**

Phonics Objectives

Can students:
- ✓ listen for the long *a* sound?
- ✓ identify the long *a* sound formed by the letter combination *ay*?
- ✓ read and write words and sentences with the long *a (ay)* sound?

Language Acquisition Objectives

Can students:
- ✓ use the verbs *play, say,* and *lay?*

ESL Standards

- Goal 2, Standard 2

DEVELOPING PHONEMIC AWARENESS

Give each student a piece of modeling clay and say, *Play with clay.* Ask students to repeat it after you and play with the clay, making something that has the long *a* sound such as *grapes,* a *plate,* or a *snake.* Ask if *play* has the same long *a* sound as *clay. (yes)* Tell students to listen carefully as you say some words. Ask them to repeat each word and, if it has the long *a* sound, play with their clay. You can use the following words: <u>day</u>, *bug,* <u>pay</u>, *big,* <u>stay</u>, <u>away</u>, *bad, sad,* <u>say</u>.

USING PAGE 31

Ask students to:
- point to the letters *ay*
- locate words as you say them
- read aloud and track words with you

Point out and read aloud the title of the page, *Kate plays.* Point out how the long *a* sound is formed in different ways in this sentence: *a-e, ay.* Which word has the long *a* sound formed by the letters *ay?* Read the first sentence in the box aloud, then ask a volunteer to find the words with the long *a* sound. Do the same with the other two sentences.

INCLUDING ALL LEARNERS

Let's Put on a Play
(Kinesthetic/Auditory Learners)

Discuss with students plays they may have seen. Divide the class into small groups and challenge them to make up a short play called "The Gray Day." Invite the groups to perform their short play for the rest of the class.

Say It!

Teach your students the following chant. 🎧

   It is such a gray (clap, clap), gray
      day (clap, clap).
   We can't go out (clap, clap), go
      out and play (clap, clap).

   It's so rainy (clap, clap), we have
      to stay (clap, clap).
   In the house (clap, clap) on this
      gray day (clap, clap).

Recite the chant as a group, then invite individual students to recite it. ✓

Write It!

Ask students to fold a piece of writing paper vertically so there are two columns. Tell them to write the word *day* on the top of one column and *Kate* on the top of the second column. Read a list of words. If the word has the long *a* sound represented by the letters *ay,* students should write the word in the column under *day.* If the word has the long *a* sound represented by the letters *a-e,* they should write the word in the column under *Kate.* Use the following words: *play, say, cake, lake, wave, lay, crayon, gray.* Allow the students to use their open books for spelling. ✓

Long Vowels: /ā/ ai

Key Words: wait, rain, hail, snail, pail, train

Phonics Objectives

Can students:
- ✓ listen for the long *a* sound?
- ✓ identify the long *a* sound formed by the letter combination *ai*?
- ✓ read and write words and sentences with the long *a* (*ai*) sound?

Language Acquisition Objectives

Can students:
- ✓ use the verb *wait*?
- ✓ use words relating to the weather?

ESL Standards

- Goal 2, Standard 2

ai — Kate waits.

It is **not** a great day.

Kate waits in the rain and hail.   a snail in a pail   train

Match the sentences with the pictures.

1. Kate waits at a bus stop in the rain.
2. Kate takes the red pail away.
3. Kate gets on the train at eight o'clock.
4. "The day is great!" says Kate.
5. Hail lands on the snail.

32 Unit 4
Long Vowels: /ā/ ai, ea, Verb: wait

BUILDING BACKGROUND

Say the words *wave* and *play,* and model oral blending: *wwwwaaaaave, plllllaaaaay.* Ask, *What do both words have in common? (the long a sound)* On the chalkboard, write the two words. Ask a volunteer to come to the board and underline the letters in each word that stand for the long *a* sound (a and e in wave, ay in play)

Tell the class that there are other ways to make the long *a* sound, too. Write the words *train* and *great* on the chalkboard. Read each word aloud, stressing the long *a* sound. Have students repeat them after you. Underline the letters *ai* in *train* and explain they they stand for the long *a* sound. Do the same with the letters *ea* in *great.*

USING PAGE 32

Ask students to:
- point to the letters *ai*
- locate words as you say them
- read aloud and track words with you

Read aloud the sentence *Kate waits.* Point out how the long *a* sound is formed in several different ways *(ay, ai, ea, a-e).* Ask a student to tell you which word has the long *a* sound formed by the letters *ai.*

INCLUDING ALL LEARNERS

Sounds Like Rain!
(Kinesthetic/Auditory Learners)

Invite students to make sounds like rain as you say some words. Ask them to repeat each word after you. If the word has the long *a* sound, they can make sounds like rain by rubbing their hands together. You can use the following words: *doll, wait, truck, train, pan, snail, even, eight, train.*

Say It!

 Teach your students the following rhyme.

What's in the mail?
Did I get a pail?
Did I get a snail?
Did I get a quail
or a great big whale?

Teach the rhyme as a group, then invite students to recite it to the class. ✓

Write It!

 Write the words *wait, snail, pail, rain, train,* and *great* on the chalkboard. Then read the following riddles to the class. After each riddle, have students write down the long *a* word that answers the riddle.

If I land on you, you will get wet. *(rain)*
You can fill me with sand. *(pail)*
You go places on me. *(train)*
You say this when you are happy. *(great)*
You sometimes do this at a bus stop. *(wait)*
I am a very slow animal. *(snail)*

Long Vowels: /ā/ *ace, age*

Key Words: face, race, page, cage, stage

Phonics Objectives

Can students:
- ✓ listen for the long *a* + soft *c* and long *a* + soft *g* sounds?
- ✓ identify the long *a* + soft *c* sounds formed by *ace* and the long *a* + soft *g* sounds formed by *age*?
- ✓ read and write words and sentences with the long *a* + soft *c* and long *a* + soft *g* sounds?

Language Acquisition Objectives

Can students:
- ✓ use the verb *have*?

ESL Standards

- Goal 2, Standard 1

ace age Kate's Face on the Page

Kate's face is happy.   Kate and Nan race.   page   cage   stage

Circle *yes* if the sentence matches the pictures above.
Circle *no* if it does not.

1. Kate has a sad face.   yes   (no)
2. The page has a cage on it.   yes   no
3. Kate and the dog race on the grass.   yes   no

The page has…/Lots of pages have…

Write the word that finishes each sentence.

1. The cage **has** a ___snake___ in it.

2. Tim and Bob **have** red _____ .

3. Kate and Nan **have** black _____ .

Long Vowels: /ā/ɑ–e; /k/ c, /s/ c, /g/ g, /j/ g; Verb: have   **Unit 4 33**

DEVELOPING PHONEMIC AWARENESS

Ask a volunteer to tell you his or her age. Then pronounce the word *age*, stressing the soft /j/ sound. Have the students repeat it after you. Point out the *a-e* pattern. Remind students that they have heard the hard /g/ sound of *g* as in *grass*. Explain that when the letter *g* appears between an *a* and an *e*, it often makes the /j/ sound. Say *age* again, stressing the /j/ sound.

Use a hand mirror to reflect a student's face and say the word *face*. Invite the class to repeat it after you. Say the word *face* and model oral blending: *fffaaaaacccce*. Point out the /s/ sound represented by the letter *c* in the word *face*. Remind students that they have learned the hard /k/ sound of *c* as in the word *cat*. Explain that when the letter *c* appears between an *a* and an *e* it often makes the /s/ sound.

USING PAGE 33

Ask students to:
- point to the letters *ace, age*
- locate words as you say them
- read aloud and track words with you

Point out the words *face* and *cage* and say them aloud. *What are the two different sounds the letter* c *makes in these words?* (/s/, /k/) Point out the words *page* and *grass* and say them aloud. *What are the two different sounds the letter* g *makes in these words?* (/j/, /g/)

Point out the word *have* on the page. Explain that *have* is used when more than one person or thing holds something.

INCLUDING ALL LEARNERS

Hold Up Your Plates!
(Auditory Learners)

Give two paper plates to each student. Instruct the class to write the letter *g* = *j* on one plate and the letter *c* = *s* on the other. Read a list of words. If the word you

read has the /j/ sound as in *age*, students should hold up the *g* plate. If the word has the /s/ sound as in *ace*, they should hold up the *c* plate. Use the following list of words: *page, pace, lace, cage, stage, place, race, rage, face*. Students can decorate their plates as happy and sad faces.

Say It!

 Teach the class the following rhyme. 🎧

> Nan races on stage.
> She reads from a page.
> Her foot taps in place.
> She has a happy face!

Which words have the /s/ sound as in ace? *Which words have the /j/ sound as in* age? ☑

Write It!

Distribute writing paper. Read the following words aloud and ask the students to write them down: *face, page, cake, race, cage, stage*. Allow the students to use their open book for spelling. ☑

Long Vowels: /ā/ and Short Vowels

Key Word: *same*

Phonics Objectives

Can students:
✓ listen for the long *a* sound?
✓ identify the long *a* sound formed by different letter combinations?
✓ read and write words and sentences with the long *a* sound?

Language Acquisition Objectives

Can students:
✓ use the contractions *it's, isn't, can't,* and *let's?*

Students:
• use similar words

ESL Standards

• Goal 1, Standard 1

It's the same.

it is	=	it's
is not	=	isn't
cannot	=	can't
let us	=	let's

Match the sentences that mean the same.

1 **It is** a great day.
2 A snake **cannot** make a cake.
3 **Let us** take a snack.
4 The snail **is not** in the pail.

a The snail **isn't** in the pail.
b **It's** a great day.
c **Let's** take a snack.
d A snake **can't** make a cake.

Two words can mean almost the same.

Read the first sentence. Finish the second sentence with the word that means almost the same.

1 A frog can **hop**. = A frog can ___**jump**___
jump/walk

2 Bob can **jog**. = Bob can _____.
swim/run

3 Kate has a **picnic**. = Kate has a _____.
snack/snake

34 Unit 4
Long Vowels /ā/a–e, ay, ea; Contractions; Similar Words

BUILDING BACKGROUND

Write the sentence *It is cold!* on the chalkboard and read it aloud, pretending you are cold. Next, write *It's cold!* Explain that *it's* means the same thing as *it is.* Explain that a *contraction* of two words is a short way of writing two words as one. On the board, write *it is* and then erase the letter *i* in *is* and substitute an apostrophe. Point to the apostrophe and say, *In contractions, this symbol takes the place of letters.* Invite students to come to the board and do more examples by erasing.

USING PAGE 34

Ask students to:
• locate the words as you say them
• read aloud and track words with you

Review the first contraction in the box, demonstrating how *it's* means the same thing as *it is.* Have the students look at the second line. Say the word *isn't* and point

out that it means the same thing as *is not.* Say a sample sentence using *isn't.* Introduce the contractions *can't* and *let's.* Then explain the similar words in the second half of the page.

INCLUDING ALL LEARNERS

Contractions Concentration
(Kinesthetic/Visual Learners)

Materials: at least 8 index cards

Students will match groups of words with their corresponding contractions. On half of the index cards, write the following: *it is, is not, cannot,* and *let us.* On the other half of the cards, write the following: *it's, isn't, can't,* and *let's.* Mix up the cards and place them facedown. Then invite two students to play the game. The first player turns over two cards. If one card has the contraction for the words on the other card, he or she can keep the cards. When all the cards have been used, the player with the most cards is the winner.

Say It!

Call on a student to hide something in the classroom. Then teach the class the following chant.

It's not here.
It's not there.
In fact, it isn't
anywhere.
I give up.
I feel blue.
I can't find it.
Hey, can you?

Ask the class to first tell you the words in the chant that are contractions and then find the hidden item. ✔

Write It!

Write the following sentences on the chalkboard. Ask the students to rewrite the sentences, replacing the underlined words with contractions.

<u>It is</u> six o'clock. *(It's)*
The man <u>is not</u> here yet. *(isn't)*
Tom <u>cannot</u> jump up. *(can't)*
<u>Let us</u> play ball. *(Let's)* ✔

Little Book: *The Lake*

Key Words: lake, Kate, wake, eight, rain, day, great, lake, take, make, lay, grapes, cake, plate, wave, play, gray, snake, race, away, wait

Phonics Objectives

Can students:
✓ listen for the short vowel and long *a* sounds?
✓ read short vowel and long *a* words in the context of a story?
✓ write words with long *a*?

Language Acquisition Objectives

Can students:
✓ read words in story context?
✓ use verbs?

ESL Standards

• Goal 1, Standard 2

Gus races in the lake, ...and the snake gets away.

The Lake

But wait!

It's not a stick.

It's a gray snake.

"Hey, Gus!" yells Kate.

"Drop the snake!"

But Gus runs and runs.

DEVELOPING PHONEMIC AWARENESS

Invite students to listen as you recite (or play) the chant below. Ask them to listen for all the long *a* sounds. You may wish to preview some of the words as you model oral blending. For example, say the word *lake: lllaaaake.*

Rain on the lake, hey!
Waves on the lake, hey!
Kate and Nan on the lake,
Great, great, great!

Invite students to recite the chant with you and then as a group on their own.

USING THE LITTLE BOOK

Explain to the students that they are going to make a Little Book about a trip to a lake. Ask them to remove pages 35 and 36 from their books. Show them how to cut the page on the dotted line with the scissors icon, then fold the pages to make their own eight-page Little Book.

Preview *The Lake* by reading the title aloud. Allow the students time to look through the book and examine the pictures. Ask the students to follow along as you read the story aloud to them.

Engage the class in the story. You can prompt the discussion by asking questions that bring in their own personal experiences and opinions, such as *Have you ever visited a lake? What kinds of things do you like to do at a lake? Do you take your pet with you? What does your pet like to do at the lake?*

Revisit the book. Lead the class in a second reading of *The Lake.* This time, ask for volunteers to read aloud one paragraph at a time. After each page is completed, ask questions about the story content. Here are some examples:

• *What do the children do at the lake?*
• *What do they take to the lake?*
• *What does Gus the dog do at the lake?*

INCLUDING ALL LEARNERS

Act Out the Story: *The Lake*
(Kinesthetic/Auditory Learners)

Materials: picnic blanket, a picnic basket, plates, a rubber snake

Ask for three volunteers to act out the story *The Lake*. Assign the roles of Kate, Nan, and Gus the dog. Students can act out the story as you read it aloud to the class. You may wish to pause at speech balloons and invite students to read the words in them.

When you are done, invite a new group of volunteers to act out the story. This time, have the other students take turns reading pages of the story while the actors perform it. Encourage other groups of students to perform the story for the class.

Story Time
(Extra Help)

Read the story aloud to the class again, but pause after each page to ask questions to check their comprehension. Here are some suggestions:

Page 2: *What do Kate and Nan want to do today? (have a picnic)*

Who do they want to take with them? (Gus the dog)

Page 4: *What does Gus do when they get to the beach? (plays with a stick)*

Page 6: *Why does Kate yell at Gus? (because he is playing with a snake)*

Page 8: *What does Gus do? (He runs in the lake.)*

What happens to the snake? (It gets away.)

Say It!

Give students time to read the story aloud. Then engage the class in a discussion about words they read in the story. *What letter sounds do you know in the words? Which words have the long a sound?* ✓

Kate and Nan wake up at eight.

The rain is gone, and the day is great.

"Let's have a picnic at the lake," says Kate.

"Great!" says Nan. "Let's take Gus."

Kate and Nan make a snack.

❷

❼

Kate takes grapes and cake.

Gus helps. Gus takes the plates.

At the lake, Nan lays the picnic on the sand.

Kate jumps in the waves.

Gus takes a stick and plays.

❹

❺

Write It!

 Write the following sentences on the chalkboard. Ask students to copy them, filling in the blanks with the correct word.

- Gus _____ a boy. (is, <u>isn't</u>)
- Nan and Kate went to the _____. (<u>lake</u>, park)
- Nan and Kate _____ Gus to the lake. (wave, <u>take</u>)
- Gus _____ with a snake. (waits, <u>plays</u>)
- The snake gets _____. (<u>away</u>, great)

When they are finished, review the activity as a class. ✓

Family Connection

Send home the Little Book *The Lake*. Encourage students to read the book to a family member.

BOOK CORNER

/ā/ ai
Bringing the Rain to Kapiti Plain
by Verna Aardema

/ā/ a-e
Wake Me in Spring
by James Preller

/ā/ a-e, ay
What Game Shall We Play?
by Pat Hutchins

/ā/ a-e /s/ c
The Big Balloon Race
by Eleanor Coerr

/j/ g
Ginger Jumps
by Lisa Campbell Ernst

Review

Long Vowels: *a* and Hard and Soft *c* and *g*

Phonics Objectives

Can students:

- ✓ listen for the long *a* sound?
- ✓ identify the long *a* sound formed by different letter combinations?
- ✓ read and write words with the long *a* sound?
- ✓ listen for the /s/ c and /j/ g in words and read words containing them?

Language Acquisition Objectives

Students:
- use verbs

ESL Standards
- Goal 1, Standard 3

Review: Kate's Great Day

Circle *yes* if the sentence matches the picture.
Circle *no* if it does not.

1. Kate and Nan play on the sand. (yes) no
2. Rain lands on the cake. yes no
3. A duck swims in the waves. yes no
4. Hail makes the day gray. yes no
5. The pail has crayons in it. yes no
6. Eight snails play on a stick. yes no
7. A train is on the page. yes no
8. The lake is gray. yes no
9. A gray snake waits on the rock. yes no
10. Kate's face is sad. yes no

Review of Long Vowels: /ā/ *a–e, ay, ea, ai;* /k/ *c,* /s/ *c,* /g/ *g,* /j/ *g;* Verbs **Unit 4 37**

DEVELOPING PHONEMIC AWARENESS

Remind the students that the long *a* sound can be formed by many different letter combinations. Say the word *snake* and model oral blending: *sssnnnaaaaake.* Say the word *snake* and ask the students to repeat it after you. Then ask them to hiss like a snake. Tell them to listen carefully as you say a list of words. Ask them to hiss like a snake when they hear the long *a* sound. Use the following words: *men, lake, rain, drain, pan, leg, crayon, fan, face, race, has.*

Ask a student to point out or name something in the classroom whose name has the long *a* sound in it. Invite other students to do the same.

USING THE REVIEW PAGE

Read "Kate's Great Day" aloud. *Which words have the long* a *sound?* Write the title on the chalkboard and ask a student to underline the letters in each word that stand for the long *a* sound. *(Kate's Great Day)* Invite the class to examine the illustration in the box. Ask, *What does the picture show?* Encourage students to point out details.

INCLUDING ALL LEARNERS

Make a Great Face Collage
(Visual Learners)

Materials: old magazines and newspapers, construction paper, tape or glue, scissors

Divide the class into pairs or small groups and distribute the materials. Ask students to find different kinds of faces in the newspapers and magazines. Encourage them to cut out the faces and make a face collage. Invite students to share their finished work with the rest of the class.

Say It!

Divide the class into pairs or small groups. Ask students to name words they know with the long *a* sound (*Kate, face, plate, grapes, cake, train, lake, page, waves, snake*). Then ask what words have the /s/ or /j/ sound. Invite them to make up their own humorous sentences using these words. ✓

Write It!

Ask students to write the words with the long *a* sound as you say them: *cake, play, wait, great,* and *eight.* Then encourage students to add, next to each word, other words they know that contain the same letter combination for the long *a* sound. ✓

UNIT 5

Long Vowels: i

Long Vowels: /ī/ *i-e*

Key Words: Mike, ride, bike, like, pie, five, nine, kite

Phonics Objectives

Can students:
- ✓ listen for the long *i* sound?
- ✓ identify the long *i* sound formed by the letter combination *i-e*?
- ✓ read and write words and sentences with the long *i* (*i-e*) sound?

Language Acquisition Objectives

Can students:
- ✓ use the verbs *ride* and *like*?
- ✓ use numbers?

ESL Standards

- Goal 2, Standard 2

UNIT 5 Long Vowels: i — i-e Mike can ride.

Mike rides a bike. Mike likes pie. five nine kite

Match the sentences with the pictures.

1. Mike rides in the rain.
2. Mike has a red kite.
3. Nan likes apple pie.
4. The time is five o'clock.
5. The page has nine lines.

a b c d e

DEVELOPING PHONEMIC AWARENESS

Say the word *five*. Ask the class to repeat the word and hold up five fingers as they orally blend the sounds. Tell students to listen carefully as you say some words. Ask them to repeat each word and, if it has the long *i* sound, hold up five fingers. You can use the following words: *big, bite, bag, mad, kite, red, hit, hide, ride, mitt, Mike.*

USING PAGE 38

Ask students to:
- point to the letters *i-e*
- locate the words as you say them
- read aloud and track words with you

Show students how the vowel *i*, a consonant, and the vowel *e* form the long *i* sound. Point out the long *i* words in the box at the top of the page that follow the VCV pattern: *Mike, rides, bike, likes, five,*

nine, kite. Explain that the long *i* sound can also be formed by other letter patterns as well. Write the word *pie* on the chalkboard.

INCLUDING ALL LEARNERS

Long or Short?
(Auditory Learners)

Materials: magazine pictures of short *i* and long *i* words such as a *bike, kite, pie, mitt*

Tell students you will show pictures of both short and long *i* words. Tell them to call out "long" if it is a picture of a long *i* word, and "short" if it is a picture of a short *i* word.

Say It!

 Teach your students the following chant.

> I like pie.
> I like kites.
> I like to ride my bike, bike, bike.

Recite the chant as a group. Let students clap when they hear the long *i* sound in

words. Invite students to add lines telling other things they like, and substitute students' names for "I", for example, *José likes fries.* ✓

Write It!

Write the words *ride, Mike, bike, like, pie, five, nine,* and *kite* on the chalkboard. Then read the following riddles to the class. After each riddle, ask students to write down the long *i* word that answers the riddle.

1. I come after the number four. *(five)*
2. You do this on a bus. *(ride)*
3. You can fly me. *(kite)*
4. You can ride me. *(bike)*
5. I am a boy's name. *(Mike)*
6. I am one less than ten. *(nine)*
7. Sometimes I have apples in me. *(pie)*
8. I rhyme with bike and Mike. *(like)*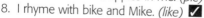

Long Vowels: /ī/ I, -y

Key Words: I, my, hi, eye, fly, sky, cry, by

I -y | I like my bike.

Hi! My bike is by the slide.

eyes/smile   A kite can fly in the sky.   cry/cries

Write the word that finishes each sentence.

1. Mike's bike is by the ___**slide**___.

2. A _____ has tires in front and back.

3. Mike says, "Hi! _____ am Mike."

4. A bike is not like a kite.

   A kite can _____ in the sky.

5. Mike's face is not sad.

   It has a big _____.

6. Mike stops and _____, "Yikes!"

front   side   back   pedal   tires

Yikes!   STOP

Long Vowels: /i/i,-y; Pronouns: I, my; Verbs: fly, cry   **Unit 5 39**

Phonics Objectives

Can students:
✓ listen for the long *i* sound?
✓ identify the long *i* sound formed by the letters *i* and *y*?
✓ read and write words and sentences with the long *i* (*I, -y*) sound?

Language Acquisition Objectives

Can students:
✓ use the pronouns *I, my?*
✓ use the verbs *fly, cry?*

ESL Standards

• Goal 2, Standard 1

Building Background

Write the capital letter *I* on the chalkboard. Explain that *I* is not only a letter but also a word that is used to refer to oneself. Invite students to say the personal pronoun *I* in other languages.

Say, *I am the teacher.* Ask students to begin a sentence with *I* and say something about themselves. Go around the class until all students have said a sentence.

Write the word *my* on the chalkboard. Pronounce it for students and let them repeat it after you. Explain that sometimes the letter *y* stands for the long *i* sound. Point to your wristwatch and say, *This is my watch.* Invite a student to hold up something of his or hers and say, *This is my _____.* Go around the room, allowing other students to say a similar sentence.

Using Page 39

Ask students to:
• point to the letters *I* and *y*
• locate the words as you say them
• read aloud and track words with you

Direct students' attention to the words *cry/cries* in the box at the top of the page. Explain that a verb that ends in *y* can express action for *I.* When the verb expresses action for another person, the *y* sometimes changes to *ies.* Write *I cry* and *Mike cries* on the chalkboard. Write some more examples on the chalkboard: *I fly, Bev flies.*

Including All Learners

Memory Game
(Visual Learners)

Materials: pictures (optional)

Ask students to draw pictures or choose pictures to show things they like. A volunteer can show his or her pictures, tell what he or she likes, and then hide the pictures. Call on students to recall all the things that the other students like: *Marie likes cake. Carl likes bikes.*

Say It!

 Teach your students the following chant.

> I'd like to fly up in the sky.
> Yes, that is what I'd like.
> But I can't fly. I'm not a kite.
> So I'll just ride my bike!

Recite the chant as a group. Ask children what long *i* words they hear. ✓

Write It!

 Dictate the following sentences to the class.

• My bike is red.
• I can fly a kite.
• I like pie.
• I cry by my bike.

When you are finished, write the sentences on the chalkboard and let students check each other's sentences for spelling. ✓

Long Vowels: /ī/ *igh*

Key Words: light, night, bright, high, right

Phonics Objectives

Can students:

✓ listen for and identify the long *i* sound formed by the letter combination *igh*?
✓ read and write words and sentences with the long *i* sound?

Language Acquisition Objectives

Can students:

✓ use the adjectives *bright, high,* and *right*?

Students:

• *left* and *right* directions
• use the verb *glide*

ESL Standards

• Goal 2, Standard 1

igh Lights at Night

bright lights at night

left/right

Wind makes the kite glide high.

Write the word that finishes each sentence.

1. Mike has bright ____lights____ on his bike.

2. Mike can ride the bike at _____.

3. A big_____ is on the front of Mike's bike.

4. The light of the sun is _____.

5. Mike's kite can glide _____ in the sky.

6. The kite is in Mike's _____ hand.

40 Unit 5
Long Vowels: /i/ *igh*; Adjectives; Directions: *left/right*; Verb: *glide*

BUILDING BACKGROUND

Write the word *hi* on the chalkboard, point to the letter *i*, and say *hi*. Next, write the word *high* next to *hi*. Pronounce the word. *How are these words alike?* Underline the letters *gh* and explain that they are silent letters–letters that we do not pronounce. Tell students that the letters *igh* stand for the long *i* sound. Write the word *light* and pronounce it. Invite students to repeat it after you. Ask a student to come to the board and underline the silent letters. Do the same with the words *bright* and *right*.

USING PAGE 40

Ask students to:

• point to the letters
• locate the words as you say them
• read aloud and track words with you

Point out the words *bright, high,* and *right* on the page. Explain that these words are adjectives, which describe things. Tell stu-

dents that the word *right* has two meanings. *Right* can mean "correct" and *right* can refer to the direction. Point out the directions *right* and *left* and explain that these directions depend on the point of view of the speaker. Face students and demonstrate that your *right* is their *left* and your *left* is their *right*.

INCLUDING ALL LEARNERS

Red Light! Green Light!
(Kinesthetic/Auditory Learners)

A volunteer stands in front of the class assembled in a line, with his or her back facing them. The volunteer repeatedly calls out *Green Light!* and students walk toward him or her. If the leader calls out *Red Light!* students stop. Anyone moving has to go back to the starting line. The student who reaches the leader first wins and is the next leader.

Say It!

Teach your students the rhyme "Star Light, Star Bright."

Star light, star bright.
First star I see tonight.
Wish I may. Wish I might.
Have the wish I wish tonight.

Teach the rhyme as a group and ask students what long *i* words they hear. ✓

Write It!

Write the following sentences on the chalkboard. Ask students to copy them, filling in the blanks with the correct word.

1. The lights were _____. (bright, night)
2. The kite is _____ in the sky. (hi, high)
3. I go to sleep at _____. (night, light)
4. Turn out the _____. (high, lights)
5. The book is in my _____ hand. (right, night) ✓

Long Vowels: /ī/ *ire, ice*

Key Words: fire, ice, tire, wide, mice, hide, bite

Phonics Objectives

Can students:
- ✓ listen for the long *i* sound *(ire, ice)*?
- ✓ identify the long *i* sound formed by *i* and *-re, -ce*?
- ✓ read and write words and sentences with the long *i* sound *(ire, ice)*?

Language Acquisition Objectives

Can students:
- ✓ use the verbs *hide* and *bite*?

ESL Standards

- Goal 1, Standard 3

---

ire | ice   Fire and Ice

ice | a wide sign | Mice bite.

fire | a flat tire | Mice hide.

Circle *yes* if the sentence is true.
Circle *no* if the sentence is not true.

1. A fire is hot.   (yes)   no
2. Mice can fly in the sky.   yes   no
3. A stop sign is red.   yes   no
4. Ice is hot.   yes   no
5. A dog can bite a ball.   yes   no
6. A kite can bite a light.   yes   no
7. Bikes have nine tires.   yes   no
8. A frog can hide in the grass.   yes   no
9. A pen is wide and big.   yes   no
10. A flat tire can make a bike stop.   yes   no

DEVELOPING PHONEMIC AWARENESS

Pronounce the word *fire* as you model oral blending and invite students to repeat it. Say the word *ice* and let students repeat that after you. Tell students they will learn about the long *i* sound in the letter combinations *ire* and *ice*. Ask students to listen as you say some words. Repeat each word and raise a piece of paper as a *sign* if they hear the sounds of *ire* or *ice*: *tire, wide, hide, mice, bite, fire, ice*.

USING PAGE 41

Ask students to:
- point to the letters *ire* and *ice*
- locate the words as you say them
- read aloud and track words with you

Write the words *bite, hide,* and *write* on the chalkboard and say them for the class.

Explain that these words all describe actions. Use gestures to explain these actions. Ask a student to name an occasion when they would *hide* or *write*.

INCLUDING ALL LEARNERS

Signs of the Times!
(Visual Learners)

Materials: old magazines or newspapers, scissors, construction paper, glue

Invite students to cut out pictures of signs in magazines and newspapers and glue them to the construction paper or make their own signs. Let them share their finished work with the rest of the class.

Say It!

Teach your students the following chant. 🎧

> Three hot and sticky mice
> Ride bikes looking for ice.
> But one of the tires goes "pop!"
> And they all have to stop!

Say the chant as a group. Ask students which words have the *ire* and *ice* sounds. ✓

Write It!

Write the words *fire, ice, tire, hide, mice,* and *bite* on the chalkboard. Then read the following riddles. After each riddle, ask students to write down the word that answers the riddle.

1. There are two on a bike. *(tire)*
2. You do this when you eat an apple. *(bite)*
3. I am very, very hot. *(fire)*
4. If you are scared, you might do this. *(hide)*
5. I am very, very cold. *(ice)*
6. They are small animals. *(mice)* ✓

Long Vowels: /ā/, /ī/ and Short Vowels

Key Word: rhymes

Phonics Objectives

Can students:
- ✓ listen for the long *a* sound and long *i* sound?
- ✓ identify the long *a* sound and long *i* sound and distinguish them from other vowel sounds?
- ✓ read and write words and sentences with the long *a* sound and long *i* sound?

Language Acquisition Objectives

Can students:
- ✓ use and identify rhymes?

ESL Standards

- Goal 2, Standard 2

Rhymes

Rhymes have the same end sounds.
Example: *Mike* and *like* rhyme.

~~lake~~	face	man	night
sky	tire	hot	run	train
yell	day	page	wide
sand	snail	class	nine	jog

Find the word from the box above that rhymes.
Write it on the line.

1. take ___lake___
2. hand _____
3. ride _____
4. race _____
5. van _____
6. light _____
7. fly _____
8. fire _____
9. line _____
10. dog _____
11. not _____
12. cage _____
13. sun _____
14. rain _____
15. bell _____
16. play _____
17. grass _____
18. pail _____

DEVELOPING PHONEMIC AWARENESS

Write the names *Jim* and *Tim* on the chalkboard. Ask a volunteer to repeat the names. *What is the same about these two names? (They both end with the same sound.)* Explain that words with the same ending sound are called *rhymes.* If any two students have names that rhyme, ask them to stand and say their names. Show Picture Cards or point out classroom objects with names that rhyme.

USING PAGE 42

Ask students to:
- point to the title "Rhymes"
- locate the words as you say them
- read aloud and track words with you

Explain that in the exercise on the page students will choose a rhyming word from the word box and write it in the blank. Tell the class that rhymes are used most often in poems and songs. You may want to bring in some recorded songs and listen to them with the class. Pause the tape or CD player every so often to discuss the rhymes used in the lyrics.

INCLUDING ALL LEARNERS

Find New Rhymes
(Auditory Learners)

Divide the class into pairs or small groups. Let them read aloud the rhyming pairs in the exercise on page 42. Then challenge them to find a third word that rhymes with each. For example, in item 1, they can add the word *make* or *snake.* Then create a master list of all the additional rhyming words they list.

Say It!

 Teach your students the following pairs of rhyming sentences.

> Are you *hot?* No I'm *not!*
> Are you *well?* I can *tell!*
> Are you *ten?* Guess *again!*
> Are you *two?* No, are *you?*

Recite each pair of rhyming sentences and ask students to identify the rhyming words. Challenge volunteers to model blending the sounds in the rhyming words. Invite students to create rhymes of their own. ✓

Write It!

Write the following words on the chalkboard: *mice, frog, cake, by, play, face, bike, make, my, hike, bright, say, night, ice, dog, race.* Tell students that each word rhymes with another word on the board. Challenge them to write each pair of rhyming words on their paper. When they are finished, review the work as a class. ✓

Little Book: *The Bike*

Key Words: bike, Mike, high, bright, wide, tire, five, light, ride, night, slide, glide, kite, fly, cry, like, mile, side, yikes

Phonics Objectives

Can students:
- ✓ listen for long *i* sounds?
- ✓ read long *i* words in the context of a story?
- ✓ write words with long *i*?

Language Acquisition Objectives

Can students:
- ✓ read words in story context?

ESL Standards
- Goal 1, Standard 2

DEVELOPING PHONEMIC AWARENESS

Invite students to listen as you recite (or play) the chant below. Ask them to listen for the long *i* sounds.

> Ride, Mike, ride!
> Ride high, ride wide.
> Ride and slide.
> Ride and glide.
> Ride, Mike, ride!

Choose some of the words from the chant to practice oral blending with the class. For example, say the word *slide: sssllliiiide.* Challenge volunteers to orally segment words from the chant by pronouncing the individual sounds that make up each word. Invite students to recite the chant with you and then as a group on their own.

USING THE LITTLE BOOK

Explain to students that they are going to make a Little Book about Mike and his bike. Ask them to remove pages 43 and 44 from their books. Show them how to cut the page on the dotted line with the scissors icon, then fold the pages to make their own eight-page Little Book.

Preview the book. Read the title *The Bike* aloud to the class. Allow students time to look through the book and examine the pictures. Ask students what they think the story will be about.

Engage the students. Ask students to follow along as you read the story aloud to them. Then read the story together as a group, while kids track with their fingers if they wish. Ask students questions about related experiences: *Do you have a bike? Does it have lights on it?*

Revisit the story. Lead the class in a second reading of *The Bike.* This time, ask for volunteers to read aloud one page at a time. After each page is completed, ask questions about the story. Here are some suggestions:

Page 2: *What color is Mike's bike? (bright red)*

Why can Mike ride his bike at night? (It has a light on it.)

Page 4: *Does Mike like to ride his bike? (yes)*

Can his bike really fly? (No, it can just go very fast.)

Page 6: *What does Gus do? (He jogs along beside Mike and his bike.)*

What happens to the bike? (It hits a rock.)

Page 8: *Why is Mike mad? (He has a flat tire.)*

INCLUDING ALL LEARNERS

Act Out the Story: *The Bike*
(Kinesthetic/Auditory Learners)

Ask for three volunteers to act out the story *The Bike.* Assign the roles of Mike, Bob, and Gus the dog. Let volunteers act out the story as you read it aloud to the class. Encourage the student playing Mike to mime riding a bike.

When you are done, invite a new group of actors to act out the story. This time, ask other students to take turns reading pages of the story while the actors perform it.

What Happens Next?
(Visual Learners)

Materials: drawing paper, markers or crayons

Ask students to make a drawing of what might happen after the last page of the story *The Bike. Does the bike get fixed? Does Mike have to walk home?* When they are finished, display the illustrations on a bulletin board.

Match Words with Pictures
(Extra Help)

Materials: photocopy of *The Bike,* large index cards, tape

Cut out the pages of *The Bike* and mount them on index cards. When you are through, you'll have some text cards and some picture cards. Place the title card and the picture cards on the chalk rail, leaving spaces between them. Hold up the first text card and read it for the class. Ask a volunteer to place the card beside the picture it describes. Continue until all the text cards have been placed. You may wish to vary the activity by placing the text cards on the chalk rail and handing students picture cards to place beside them.

Mike sits high on his bike.

It's a bright, red bike.

Mike can ride fast and race on it.

It has wide, black tires and blue pedals.

On the back, it has five little lights.

Mike can ride his bike day and night.

The bike can race up hills and slide on sand.

It can glide like a kite.

"My bike can fly!" cries Mike.

"I can ride like the wind. I can race day and night. I can ride miles and miles!"

Say It!

 Give students time to read the story aloud. Then engage the class in a discussion about words they read in the story. *What letter sounds do you know in the words? Which words have the long i sound?* ✔

Write It!

Challenge students to look through their Little Book and make a list of all the names and words that have the long *i* sound in them. When they are finished, they can review their words in pairs. ✔

Family Connection

Send home the Little Book *The Bike.* Encourage students to read the book to a family member.

BOOK CORNER

/ī/ i-e
The Bike Lesson
by Stan and Jan Berenstain

/ī/ i-e
Fire! Fire! Said Mrs. McGuire
by Bill Martin, Jr.

/ī/ i-e, -y
If Mice Could Fly
by John Cameron

/ī/ igh
Night Sounds, Morning Colors
by Rosemary Wells

/ī/ igh, i-e
Tight Times by Barbara Hazen

/ī/ i, -y
Why Can't I Fly?
by Rita Golden Gelman

Review

Long Vowels: *a, i* and Short Vowels

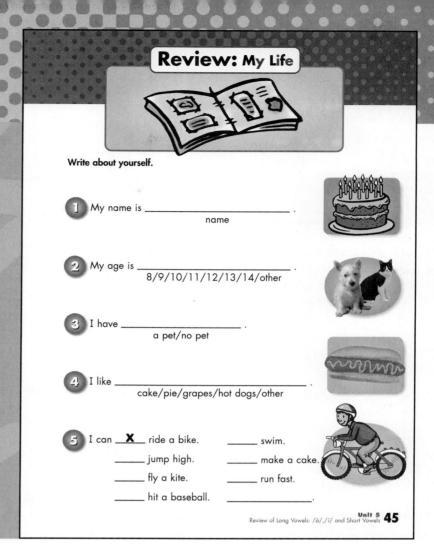

Review: My Life

Write about yourself.

1. My name is _____ .

name

2. My age is _____ .

8/9/10/11/12/13/14/other

3. I have _____ .

a pet/no pet

4. I like _____ .

cake/pie/grapes/hot dogs/other

5. I can __X__ ride a bike. _____ swim.

_____ jump high. _____ make a cake.

_____ fly a kite. _____ run fast.

_____ hit a baseball. _____

Review of Long Vowels: /ā/,/ī/ and Short Vowels   **Unit 5** **45**

BUILDING BACKGROUND

Go around the class, and ask each student what his or her favorite food is. Write their answers on the chalkboard. When everyone has shared, review the results of the survey.

Explain that there are all sorts of ways for a person to describe himself or herself. Go around the room again and invite students to say something about themselves. This can include their age, hair color, birthday, favorite food, favorite pet. Tell the class that in the next activity they will be filling in a scrapbook page with information about themselves.

USING THE REVIEW PAGE

Read "My name is" aloud to the class and then ask students to write their full names on the line. Explain to them that for the remaining sentences on the page they can either choose from the answer choices or write their own answers. Point out where the word "other" appears and tell them that this means they can write things that are not listed there as choices.

INCLUDING ALL LEARNERS

Filling out Forms
(Visual Learners)

Bring in copies of a simple application form for something such as a library card. Distribute them to the class, read them aloud, and then model for students how to fill in the required information.

Say It!

Let students work in pairs to create sentences with a word or words that have the long *i* sound. Each partner can take turns reciting his or her sentences while the other partner listens and identifies the words with the long *i* sound. ✓

Write It!

On the chalkboard, write the title "I Like. . . . " Distribute the drawing materials and ask students to write "I Like . . . " on the top of their paper. Then, ask them to list four or five things that they like. When they are finished, invite students to share their work with the class. ✓

UNIT 6

Long Vowels: o, e, u

Long Vowels: /ō/ o-e, oa

Key Words: Rose, goat, rope, nose, boat, float, soap

Phonics Objectives

Can students:
- ✓ listen for the long *o* sound?
- ✓ identify the long *o* sound formed by the letter combinations *o-e* and *oa*?
- ✓ read and write words and sentences with the long *o* sound *(o-e, oa)*?

Language Acquisition Objectives

Can students:
- ✓ use the verbs *hold* and *float*?

ESL Standards
- • Goal 2, Standard 1

UNIT 6 Long Vowels: o, e, u **o-e** **oa** Rose is a goat.

A rope holds Rose's nose.

Rose is a goat. Boats float. soap SOAP

Match the sentences with the pictures.

1. Rose walks in the road.
2. Rose is by the boat.
3. Rose has a little goat.
4. The soap floats.
5. A rope is on Rose's nose.

Rose

a
b
c
d
e SOAP

46 Unit 6
Long Vowels: /ō/ o-e, oa; Verbs: hold, float

DEVELOPING PHONEMIC AWARENESS

Say the word *nose,* stressing the long *o* sound, and point to your nose. Say the word again and model oral blending: *nnnoooooossse.* Have the class repeat it after you. Explain that the long *o* sound can be formed by different letter groups that they will learn about.

Tell students to listen carefully as you say some words. Ask them to repeat each word and, if it has the long *o* sound, point to their noses. You can use the following words: *bed, soap, game, goat, boat, hold, cat, rope, nose, cage, float.*

USING PAGE 46

Ask students to:
- • point to the letters *o-e* and *oa*
- • locate the words as you say them
- • read aloud and track words with you

Write *nose* and *soap* on the chalkboard and explain that these words have the same long *o* sound, but it is spelled in different ways: *o-e, oa.*

Then point out *float* and *hold* on the page. Explain that these are action words called verbs. Pick up a pen and say, *I can hold the pen.* Pass the pen to a student and have him or her say the sentence. Students can pass the pen around for everyone to say the sentence. Then review other action words students know.

INCLUDING ALL LEARNERS

The Long *o* Road
(Kinesthetic/Visual Learners)
Materials: construction paper, drawing paper, markers, chalk, tape or tacks

Ask the class to draw pictures of things with the long *o* sound in their names. Then let students create a road on the bulletin board using black construction paper and chalk, and tack or tape their long *o* drawings along the road.

Say It!

 Teach the following chant.

> Rose is a goat
> She walks in the road.
> She rides in a boat.
> And she can float, float, float!

Ask students to clap every time they hear a word with the long *o* sound. ✓

Write It!

 Write *boat, nose, float, rope,* and *soap* on the chalkboard. Read the following riddles and ask students to write the long *o* word answers. To make the activity easier, show picture cues for the answers.

1. You can hold and climb up me. *(rope)*
2. You get clean with me. *(soap)*
3. A boat does this. *(float)*
4. You smell with me. *(nose)*
5. You can sail me on a lake. *(boat)*

Long Vowels: /ō/ ow

Key Words: slow, grow, blow, window

Phonics Objectives

Can students:
- ✓ listen for the long *o* sound?
- ✓ identify the long *o* sound formed by the letter combination *ow*?
- ✓ read and write words and sentences with the long *o* sound (*ow*)?

Language Acquisition Objectives

Can students:
- ✓ use the verbs *grow, blow*?
- ✓ use the adjectives *fast, slow*?
- ✓ use weather words?

ESL Standards
- Goal 2, Standard 2

o **ow** Go Fast/Go Slow

Plants grow. cold snow

fast boat/slow boat   Winds blow.   window

Write the word that finishes each sentence.

1 A rowboat is a _____**slow**_____ boat.

2 Rose walks in the _____ and gets cold.

3 Cold winds _____ on the lake.

4 The desk is by the _____ .

5 Plants _____ in the sun.

Long Vowels: /ō/o, ow; Verbs: grow, blow; Adjectives **Unit 6 47**

DEVELOPING PHONEMIC AWARENESS

Say very, very slowly, *Hello, students. I am very glad to see all of you.* Ask the class to say how you were speaking. *(slowly)* Say the word *slow* and model oral blending: *sssllllloooow.* Then ask if the word *slow* has the long *o* sound. Tell students that *slow* is the opposite of *fast*. Invite students to brainstorm things that are slow and things that are fast.

Ask students to jog in place listening carefully as you say some words. If the word has the long *o* sound as in the word *slow*, they should slow down and jog very slowly. If the word does not have the long *o* sound, they should speed up. Use the following words: *plate, blow, grapes, grow, know, nod, bus, crow, show, hit.*

USING PAGE 47

Ask students to:
- point to the letters *ow*
- locate the words as you say them
- read aloud and track words with you

Ask students to find the words *snow, cold,* and *blow* on the page. Explain that these words can be used to describe the weather. Brainstorm other words the students know that could be used to describe the weather. *(rain, sunshine, hot, wind)*

INCLUDING ALL LEARNERS

Snow Windows
(Kinesthetic Learners)

Materials: white drawing paper or lace doilies, scissors, tape

Distribute the drawing paper or lace doilies and ask students to cut them into snowflake designs. Then decorate the windows with the snowflakes.

Say It!

 Teach the song "Row, Row, Row Your Boat."

> Row, row, row your boat
> Gently down the stream.
> Merrily, merrily, merrily, merrily
> Life is but a dream.

Show students how to sing it as a round, using gestures for rowing, a stream flowing, and dreaming. ✓

Write It!

Write *grow, slow, blow* on the chalkboard. Read aloud the following riddles and ask students to write the long *o* word answers.

1. I'm not very fast, you know. I am very, very _____. *(slow)*
2. I am tossed to and fro when I feel the cold wind _____. *(blow)*
3. Put your plants by the window, water them, and watch them _____. *(grow)* ✓

Long Vowels: /ō/ or, oor, oar, our

Key Words: more, sport, door, floor, scoreboard, corn, four, fork

Phonics Objectives

Can students:
- ✓ listen for the long o sound?
- ✓ identify the long o sound formed by the letter combinations or, oor, oar, our?
- ✓ read and write words and sentences with the long o sound (or, oor, oar, our)?

Language Acquisition Objectives

Can students:
- ✓ use the adjective more?

ESL Standards

- Goal 2, Standard 1

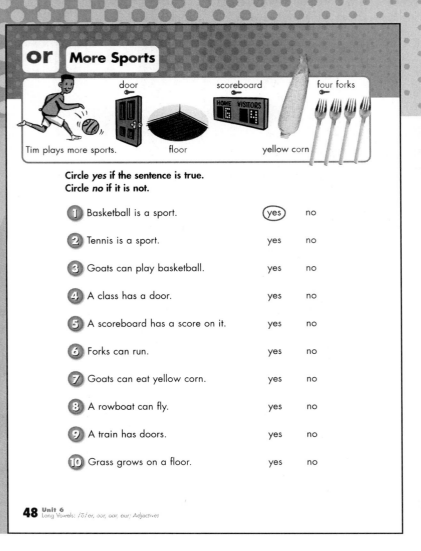

or More Sports

door   scoreboard   four forks

Tim plays more sports.   floor   yellow corn

Circle *yes* if the sentence is true.
Circle *no* if it is not.

1. Basketball is a sport.   (yes)   no
2. Tennis is a sport.   yes   no
3. Goats can play basketball.   yes   no
4. A class has a door.   yes   no
5. A scoreboard has a score on it.   yes   no
6. Forks can run.   yes   no
7. Goats can eat yellow corn.   yes   no
8. A rowboat can fly.   yes   no
9. A train has doors.   yes   no
10. Grass grows on a floor.   yes   no

BUILDING BACKGROUND

Ask two volunteers to come to the front of the class. Hand student 1 four pens, and student 2 six pens. Say, *(student 1's name) has four pens.* Ask the class to say it with you. Then say, *(student 2's name) has more pens.* Ask the class to say it with you. Ask students to switch pens. Invite volunteers to say the two sentences, reflecting who has four pens and who has more pens. Point out that the words *four* and *more* have the same long o sound with the letter *r.*

USING PAGE 48

Ask students to:
- point to the letters *or, oor, oar, our*
- locate the words as you say them
- read aloud and track words with you

Point out the red letters of the words in the box. Read aloud each of the words, emphasizing the /ō/ sound: *more, sports, door, floor, scoreboard, corn, four, forks.* Ask, *How is the /ō/ sound in these words different from the /ō/ sound in the word* snow? Explain that these words all have the long o sound influenced by the sound of the *r.* Brainstorm with students other words they know that have this sound and make a list on the chalkboard.

INCLUDING ALL LEARNERS

Door Decorations
(Visual Learners)

Materials: magazines and newspapers, scissors, tape

Distribute materials and ask students to cut out four different pictures of doors. Invite the class to decorate a door in the classroom with the door pictures.

Say It!

 Teach the class the following rhyme. 🎧

> The baseball score was four to four.
> The crowd began to roar.
> Then they scored another four.
> But we came back with more.

Recite the rhyme as a class and ask students which words contain the /ōr/ sound. ✓

Write It!

Instruct students to divide their paper into two columns and label them FOUR and MORE. Ask students to write four words with /ōr/ in the first column, and more than four words with /ōr/ in the second column. Let students refer to their Student Books. Review finished work as a class. ✓

Long Vowels: /ō/ and Short Vowels

Key Word: low

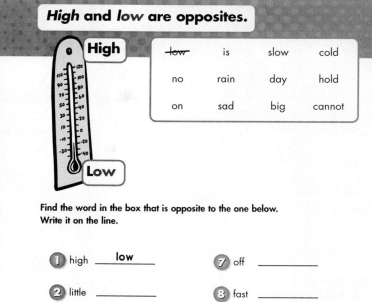

High and low are opposites.

~~low~~	is	slow	cold
no	rain	day	hold
on	sad	big	cannot

Find the word in the box that is opposite to the one below.
Write it on the line.

1. high   __low__
2. little _____
3. yes _____
4. hot _____
5. can _____
6. is not _____

7. off _____
8. fast _____
9. sun _____
10. drop _____
11. night _____
12. glad _____

Phonics Objectives

Can students:
- ✓ listen for the long *o* sound?
- ✓ identify the long *o* sound formed by different letter combinations?
- ✓ read and write words and sentences with the long *o* sound?

Language Acquisition Objectives

Can students:
- ✓ use opposites?

ESL Standards
- Goal 2, Standard 2

BUILDING BACKGROUND

Draw a happy face and a sad face on the chalkboard. Ask a volunteer to identify the emotions shown in the faces and then show these emotions in his or her own face. Explain that *happy* and *sad* are opposites. As another example of opposites, write *high* at the top of the chalkboard and *low* at the bottom. Ask a volunteer to point out an object that is high and an object that is low in the room. Then say the following words, and ask the class to come up with their opposites: *yes (no), hot (cold), near (far), up (down), dirty (clean)*.

USING PAGE 49

Ask students to:
- point to the letters *ow*
- locate the words as you say them
- read aloud and track words with you

Bring a thermometer to class and explain that it measures temperature. Point out that the words *high* and *low* on the thermometer on the page refer to the temperature level. Open a newspaper to the weather section and read aloud the high and low temperatures for yesterday. You may want to ask students to keep a graph of daily temperatures over a few days or weeks, noting the high and low temperatures.

INCLUDING ALL LEARNERS

Opposites Display
(Visual Learners)

Materials: old magazines or newspapers, scissors, tacks or tape

Divide the class into groups and challenge them to draw or find pictures of things that are opposite. Have them cut out the pictures. When each group has found three or four opposite pairs such as

hot/cold, tall/short, big/little, invite students to tack them to the bulletin board to make an "Opposites Display."

Say It!

Pair students and ask each pair to create an oral sentence that has two words with opposite meanings. Invite the pairs to share their sentences with the class and ask the class to check their opposites. ✓

Write It!

Write these words on the chalkboard: *fast, happy, night, hot, yes, little, cannot.* Read aloud the following words and ask students to write down the opposite of each word as you say it: *sad, big, slow, no, cold, can, day.* When you are finished, review the work as a class. ✓

Long Vowels: /ē/ e-e, ea, ee

Key Words: Pete, read, sleep, tree, team, eat, meat, green, leaf, feet

Phonics Objectives

Can students:
- ✓ listen for the long e sound?
- ✓ identify the long e sound formed by the letter combinations e-e, ea, ee?
- ✓ read and write words and sentences with the long e sound (e-e, ea, ee)?

Language Acquisition Objectives

Can students:
- ✓ use the verbs *read, sleep,* and *eat?*

ESL Standards

- Goal 2, Standard 1

e-e ea ee **Pete reads by the tree.**

He sleeps by a tree.

green leaf

Pete reads.

The team eats meat.

feet

Match the sentences with the pictures.

1. Pete reads a lot.
2. He is on the green team.
3. The tree has yellow leaves.
4. Gus eats Pete's meat.
5. Pete sleeps till nine o'clock.

DEVELOPING PHONEMIC AWARENESS

Point to something green and say, *I see something green.* Ask volunteers to name green things they see. Point out the /ē/ sound in *see* and *green.* Explain that the long e sound is formed by different groups of letters such as *e-e, ea, ee.*

Point to your feet and say, *feet.* Say the word *feet* again and model oral blending: *fffeeeeet.* Tell students to listen as you say some words. Ask them to repeat each word and if it has the long e sound, they should stamp their feet. You can use the following words: <u>heat</u>, hat, mat, <u>meat</u>, <u>sleep</u>, <u>treat</u>, boat, grape, <u>green</u>, <u>neat</u>, time, <u>team</u>.

USING PAGE 50

Ask students to:
- point to the letters *e-e, ea,* and *ee*
- locate the words as you say them
- read aloud and track words with you

Point out the words *read, sleep,* and *eat* on the page and read them aloud. Explain that these are action words with the long e sound. Engage the students in a discussion on when they *read, sleep,* and *eat* things.

INCLUDING ALL LEARNERS

The Long e Tree
(Visual Learners)

Materials: green and brown construction paper, drawing paper, markers or crayons, chalk, scissors, tape or tacks

Distribute green construction paper and scissors. Ask students to cut out large leaf shapes and draw on each leaf a picture of something with the long e sound in its name. Create a tree on the bulletin board out of brown construction paper and ask students to tack or tape their long e leaves to the branches.

Say It!

 Teach the following rhyme.

Meet my feet.
Meet my feet.
Left and right—they can't be beat!
See my feet.
See my feet.
Left and right—they're really neat!

Ask students to stomp their feet every time they hear the long e sound. ✓

Write It!

Write *read, sleep, tree, meat, feet* on the chalkboard. Read the class the following riddles. Ask students to write the long e word answers.

1. You do this all night long. *(sleep)*
2. You have two of them. *(feet)*
3. You do this with a book. *(read)*
4. I am tall and full of leaves. *(tree)*
5. You can eat this for dinner. *(meat)*

Long Vowels: /ē/ *ie*
Key Word: field

Phonics Objectives
Can students:
✓ listen for the long *e* sound?
✓ identify the long *e* sound formed by the letter combination *ie*?
✓ read and write words and sentences with the long *e* sound (*e, ie*)?

Language Acquisition Objectives
Can students:
✓ use the prepositions *behind, beside, in front of, in back of, above, between, below*?

ESL Standards
• Goal 1, Standard 3

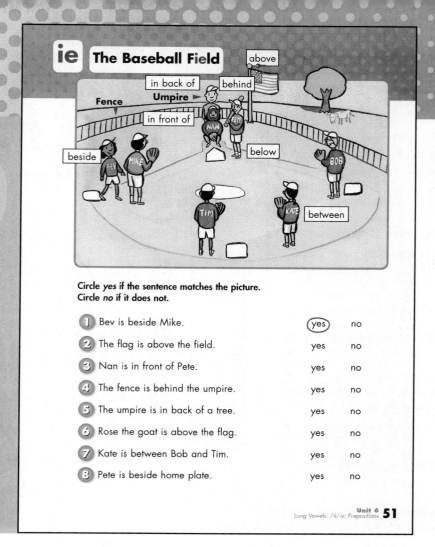

ie   The Baseball Field

Circle *yes* if the sentence matches the picture.
Circle *no* if it does not.

 Bev is beside Mike.   (yes)   no

2 The flag is above the field.   yes   no

3 Nan is in front of Pete.   yes   no

4 The fence is behind the umpire.   yes   no

5 The umpire is in back of a tree.   yes   no

6 Rose the goat is above the flag.   yes   no

7 Kate is between Bob and Tim.   yes   no

 Pete is beside home plate.   yes   no

BUILDING BACKGROUND

Write *behind, in front of, beside* on the chalkboard. Stand behind your desk and say, *I am behind my desk.* Step in front of your desk and say, *I am in front of my desk.* Then step to the side of your desk and say, *I am beside my desk.* Invite students to repeat each sentence with you as they step behind, in front of, and beside their own desks.

Divide the class into partners, each pair using an object to practice prepositions. One student puts the object somewhere and asks his or her partner, *Where is it?* The partner should answer using the prepositions he or she knows. Then ask partners to switch roles.

USING PAGE 51

Ask students to:
• point to the letters *ie*
• locate the words as you say them
• read aloud and track words with you

Read aloud the title of the page, *The Baseball Field,* and point out the long *e* sound in *field.* Explain the prepositions in the baseball field scene: *Nan is* in front of *the umpire. The umpire is* in back of/behind *Nan. Mike is* beside *Bev. Kate is* between *Tim and Bob. The field is* below *the flag. The flag is* above *the field.* Then ask, *Who likes to play baseball? Do you have favorite players or teams?* Encourage discussion for students to expand their oral language.

INCLUDING ALL LEARNERS

Listen and Draw
(Visual/Auditory Learners)

Materials: markers, drawing paper

Ask students to listen and draw as you read the following directions: *In the middle of the page, draw a tree. Draw a bird above the tree. Draw a cat beside the tree. Draw a dog in front of the tree. Draw a sun above the tree.*

Say It!

Teach the class the following rhyme.

> The sky is high above my head.
> Below me are my feet.
> Behind me is the big red sun.
> Beside me is the street.

Ask students to demonstrate the prepositions as they say them. Ask which words have the long *e* sound. ✓

Write It!

Materials: pictures of long *e* words

Display pictures of the long *e* words in different positions. Write the prepositions on the board and then ask questions about the pictures using the prepositions (*behind, in front of, beside, below, between, in back of,* and *above*). Have students write the answers to your questions. ✓

Long Vowels: /ē/ e, ey, y
Key Words: monkey, donkey, happy, baby, puppy, twenty, he, me

e **ey** Is he a monkey? **y** Is he a baby?

He likes me.

monkey   donkey   happy baby   puppy   twenty

20

Write the word or words from above that answer the riddle.

1. He smiles a lot. He likes milk.
   He plays on a mat. He is a ___happy baby___.

2. He is big and gray. He has four legs.
   He likes grass. He is a _____.

3. He has four little legs. He can play ball.
   He likes bones. He is a _____.

bone

4. It is the same as six and six and eight.
   It is _____.

5. He plays in trees. He can jump high. He has feet and
   hands. He likes bananas. He is a _____.

bananas

52 Unit 6
Long Vowels: /ē/ e, ey, y; Pronouns: he, me

DEVELOPING PHONEMIC AWARENESS

Tell students to listen carefully as you say the following words: *happy, baby, monkey. What sound do these words have in common?* Explain that sometimes *y* or *ey* stand for the long e sound that they hear at the end of these words.

Distribute sheets of paper and ask each student to draw a happy face. Say a list of words. Ask the class to repeat each word, and hold up their happy faces if the word has the long e sound. You can use these words: *monkey, rabbit, baby, button, money, funny, Monday, open, puppy.*

USING PAGE 52

Ask students to:
- point to the letters e, ey, and y
- locate the words as you say them
- read aloud and track words with you

Point out the pronouns *he* and *me* on the page. Write, *Pete likes cake* on the board. Erase *Pete* and write *He* in its place. Explain that *he* can take the place of a boy's name in a sentence. Write simple sentences using first names of boys in the class. Invite students to erase the name, write *he* in its place, and read the new sentence aloud. Then write *me* on the chalkboard. Hand a student a ruler and say, *Please give the ruler to me.* Let another student ask you for the ruler, using the word *me* and taking the ruler. Continue until everyone has said the sentence with the word *me*.

INCLUDING ALL LEARNERS

Happy Me!
(Visual/Auditory Learners)

Materials: drawing paper, markers

Distribute drawing materials and invite students to draw pictures of things that make them happy. Ask students to present their drawings using the sentence _____ *makes me happy*.

Say It!

 Teach the class the following chant. 🎧

> I see a happy monkey.
> He hops from tree to tree.
> He's having fun.
> Just see him run!
> Will he hop to me?

Recite the chant together and ask students to hop when they say a long e word. ✓

Write It!

Write the following sentences on the board. Ask students to copy the sentences, then cross out each name and replace it with the word *he*.

1. Ted is a baby.
2. Bongo is a monkey.
3. Paul sees a donkey.

Long Vowels: /ē/ eer, ear

Key Words: deer, near, ear, hear, clear, year

Phonics Objectives

Can students:
- ✓ listen for the long e sound?
- ✓ identify the long e sound formed by the letter combinations eer and ear?
- ✓ read and write words and sentences with the long e sound (eer, ear)?

Language Acquisition Objectives

Can students:
- ✓ use the verbs hear and see?
- ✓ use the adjectives near and clear?

ESL Standards

- Goal 2, Standard 1

---

eer **ear** **The deer is near.**

Pete's ears can hear.   He is fourteen years old.

The deer is near.   A nice clear sky

Write the word that finishes each sentence.

1. The ____deer____ sees a fox.

2. The fox has big _____ .
   It can hear the deer.

3. The sun is bright and the sky is _____ .

4. Nan is ten _____ old.

5. The puppy sits _____ Pete.

DEVELOPING PHONEMIC AWARENESS

Ask one student to tell you his or her age. Then say, *(student's name) is (age) years old.* Ask if *year* has the long e sound. Go around the class and let everyone say how old he or she is with the sentence *I am ___ years old.*

Say the word *ears* slowly blending the sounds of the letters while cupping your ears. Ask students to listen as you say words and repeat each after you. If the word has the long e sound like in *ears,* they should cup their ears as they say it. Use the following words: <u>dear</u>, door, <u>fear</u>, tire, fire, <u>beard</u>, <u>clear</u>, <u>near</u>, floor, more, <u>hear</u>.

USING PAGE 53

Ask students to:
- point to the letters *eer* and *ear*
- locate the words as you say them
- read aloud and track words with you

Point out the words *near* and *clear* on the page and say them aloud, stressing the long e sound. Explain that these words, called adjectives, describe things. Ask students to name things that are *near* the school. Then write a list on the board of other adjectives they know.

INCLUDING ALL LEARNERS

Near and Not Near Game
(Kinesthetic/Auditory Learners)

Tell a volunteer that you are thinking of something or someone in the classroom and to try to figure out what or who it is. Tell the student to move in any direction. If he or she moves closer to the item you selected, say *near*. If he or she moves away from it, say *not near*. The student continues to move as you give *near* and *not near* clues until the object or person is discovered. Then ask for two volunteers—one to pick an object and give clues and one to hunt for the object.

Say It!

Put students into two groups (A and B) and teach the following chant.

A: What do you hear
in your ear, ear, ear?

B: I hear a bug!
Now what do you hear?
Now what do you hear
In your ear, ear, ear?

A: I hear a frog near.
Now what do you hear?

Encourage students to make up their own verses. ✓

Write It!

Write the words *deer, ears, hear, clear* on the chalkboard. Read the following riddles to the class and ask students to write down the long e word answers.

1. This animal lives in the woods. *(deer)*
2. Glass in a window is this. *(clear)*
3. You have two on your head. *(ears)*
4. You do this with your ears. *(hear)* ✓

Long Vowels: /ü/ ue, u-e

Key Words: Sue, tune, flute, use, blue, glue, huge, cube, music

Phonics Objectives

Can students:
- ✓ listen for the long *u* sound?
- ✓ identify the long *u* sound formed by the letter combinations *ue, u-e*?
- ✓ read and write words and sentences with the long *u* sound (*ue, u-e*)?

Language Acquisition Objectives

Can students:
- ✓ use words relating to music: *tune, flute*?
- ✓ use the verb *use*?

ESL Standards
- Goal 2, Standard 1

ue u-e **Sue plays the flute.**

Sue plays a tune on the flute.

music

a huge cube

Sue uses a blue pen and glue.

Match the sentences with the pictures.

1. Sue plays the flute.
2. Sue has huge blue eyes.
3. Sue has a blue bike.
4. Sue uses the glue.
5. The glass has ice cubes in it.

54 Unit 6
Long Vowels /ü/ue, u-e, Verb: use

DEVELOPING PHONEMIC AWARENESS

Hold up a blue sheet of paper and say the word *blue,* stressing the long *u* sound. Say the word *blue* again more slowly as you model blending the sounds of *bl* and *ue: bluuuue.* Tell the class that the /ü/ sound in *blue* is called the long *u* sound. Point out that the /ū/ sound in *huge cube* is a slight variation of the long *u* sound. Say the word *huge* and model oral blending: *huuuuge.* Explain that the long *u* sound can be formed by different letter groups.

Hand out a piece of blue paper to each student. Ask them to listen carefully as you say some words. Ask them to repeat each word and, if it has the long *u* sound like in *blue* or *cube,* they should wave their blue papers over their head. You can use the following words: *fly, flute, hug, huge, cube, tug, tube, sand, Sue, cat, cut, cute.*

USING PAGE 54

Ask students to:
- point to the letters *ue, u-e*
- locate the words as you say them
- read aloud and track words with you

Hum a familiar tune for the class, then ask if anyone can identify the *tune.* Point out the picture and the sentence *Sue plays a tune on the flute* on the page. Explain that *tune* is another word for song or melody. Tell students that you *use* a flute to play a tune. Pretend to play a flute as you say the word *flute.* If anyone in the class plays the flute or a small instrument, invite her or him to bring it to class.

Point out the red letters in the words in the box on the page and explain how *ue* and *u-e* both stand for the long *u* sound.

INCLUDING ALL LEARNERS

Sharing Tunes
(Auditory Learners)

Hum a familiar tune such as "Happy Birthday to You" and ask students to guess the name of the song. The first one to guess gets to hum a tune of his or her own while classmates try to guess it.

Say It!

 Teach the following rhyme. 🎧

> When I play upon my flute,
> It is such a treat.
> I play my tunes
> From May till June
> And dance with both my feet!

Invite students to pretend to play a flute as they say the rhyme. ✔

Write It!

Dictate the following long *u* words for the students to write down: *flute, blue, tune, use, glue, huge, cube.* Review their work as a class. ✔

ou Do you...?

Do you like soup?

Yes, I do.

No, I do not (don't).

juice   Two groups of fruit

2

Circle *yes* if you do. Circle *no* if you do not.

1 Do you like fruit? (Yes, I do.) No, I don't.

2 Do you like grape juice? Yes, I do. No, I don't.

3 Do you like to play baseball? Yes, I do. No, I don't.

4 Do you walk to class? Yes, I do. No, I don't.

5 Do you have a dog? Yes, I do. No, I don't.

6 Do you have a blue pen? Yes, I do. No, I don't.

7 Do you have a cat? Yes, I do. No, I don't.

8 Do you help in class? Yes, I do. No, I don't.

9 Do you play basketball? Yes, I do. No, I don't.

10 Do you sit in the front of the class? Yes, I do. No, I don't.

Long Vowels /ü/ ou, ui; Pronoun you; Questions with do you; Contraction: don't **Unit 6 55**

Phonics Objectives

Can students:
✓ listen for and identify the long *u* sound formed by the letter combinations *ou* and *ui*?
✓ read and write words and sentences with the long *u* sound?

Language Acquisition Objectives

Can students:
✓ use the pronoun *you*?
✓ respond to questions beginning with *Do you . . . ?*
✓ use the contraction *don't*?

ESL Standards
• Goal 1, Standard 1

BUILDING BACKGROUND

Ask the class, *When you meet new friends, how do you find out about them?* Write *Do you . . .* on the chalkboard and say it aloud. Ask them to repeat it. Explain that questions beginning with *Do you . . .* are an excellent way to find out about people.

Ask a student, *Do you like sports?* Explain that you can answer *Yes, I do* or *No, I do not.* Point out that another way to say *do not* is to use the contraction *don't.* After the student has answered, have him or her ask another student the same question. Continue until all the students have asked and answered the question.

USING PAGE 55

Ask students to:
• point to the letters *ou, ui*
• locate the words as you say them
• read aloud and track words with you

Point out to students how the letters *ou* and *ui* form the /ü/ sound in words such as *you* on the page. Explain that *you* is a pronoun, like *he* and *me* that the students learned earlier. Tell the class that when they are talking directly to someone, they use *you* instead of the person's name. Then demonstrate pronouns by pointing at self (me), at another (you), at a boy (him), at a girl (her), and at self and another (us).

INCLUDING ALL LEARNERS

Find Out about Someone
(Extra Help)

Brainstorm with the class different *Do you . . .* questions that you could ask people to find out about them. Write their suggestions on the chalkboard. Create a questionnaire or interview chart with their questions. Provide answer lines for students to write *yes* or *no.* Ask students to complete the questionnaires and review the results as a class.

Say It!

Divide the class into two groups: A and B. Then teach them the following chant.

A: Oops! Oops!
B: What did you do?
A: I spilled my juice.
B: Too bad for you!

Tell Group A to brainstorm different answers for *What did you do?* Then switch groups. ✓

Write It!

Ask students to write the following questions on their paper as you dictate them and then write *Yes, I do* or *No, I don't* answers: *Do you like juice? Do you like fruit? Do you like soup?* ✓

Long Vowels: /ū/ ew

Key Words: new, few

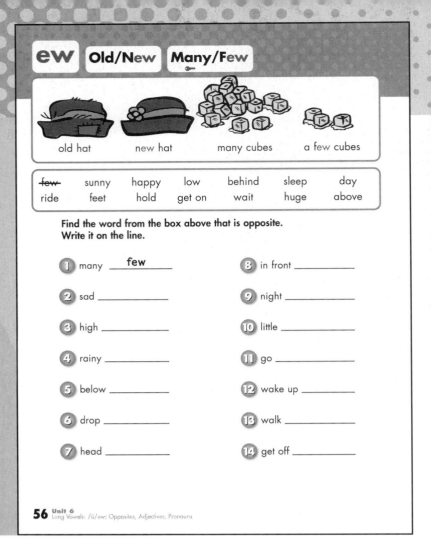

ew | **Old/New** | **Many/Few**

old hat   new hat   many cubes   a few cubes

| ~~few~~ | sunny | happy | low | behind | sleep | day |
| ride | feet | hold | get on | wait | huge | above |

**Find the word from the box above that is opposite.
Write it on the line.**

1. many   **few**
2. sad _____
3. high _____
4. rainy _____
5. below _____
6. drop _____
7. head _____
8. in front _____
9. night _____
10. little _____
11. go _____
12. wake up _____
13. walk _____
14. get off _____

56 Unit 6
Long Vowels: /ū/ ew; Opposites, Adjectives, Pronouns

Phonics Objectives

Can students:
✓ listen for and identify the long *u* sound formed by the letter combination *ew*?
✓ read and write words and sentences with the long *u* sound?

Language Acquisition Objectives

Can students:
✓ use opposites: *old/new* and *many/few*?

Students:
• review adjectives

ESL Standards

• Goal 2, Standard 3

DEVELOPING PHONEMIC AWARENESS

Pronounce the words *new, few, cubes* slowly, stressing the /ū/ sound. Ask students to repeat the words. Then say the words *Sue, flute, soup,* stressing the /ü/ sound, and ask students to repeat them. *What are the different long* u *sounds?* (/ū/ *and* /ü/) Explain that the /ū/ sound begins with the sound of *y.*

USING PAGE 56

Ask students to:
• point to the letters *ew*
• locate the words as you say them
• read aloud and track words with you

Point out the opposite pairs in the title of the page. Hold up a new item and say the word *new.* Hold up an old item and say the word *old.* Explain that *new* and *old* are opposites. Then display a tall stack of books and a very small stack of books. Put your hand on the tall stack and say *many.* Put your hand on the short stack and say *few.* Tell students that *few* and *many* describe the number of things as adjectives and also stand alone as pronouns. Then explain that *few* and *many* are opposites. Review opposites that students have learned, for example, *high/low, yes/no, happy/sad,* and *hot/cold.*

INCLUDING ALL LEARNERS

Using Glue
(Visual Learners)

Materials: magazines or newspapers, scissors, glue, construction paper

Divide the class into pairs or small groups and distribute the materials. Ask students to find pictures of similar items that are old and new, cut them out, and paste them on their paper.

Say It!

 Teach the following traditional rhyme from England. 🎧

Something old
Something new
Something borrowed
Something blue
Silver sixpence in your shoe.

Explain that this rhyme tells how a bride is supposed to dress when she gets married. Ask students about wedding ceremonies in other countries. Point out that a sixpence is a coin from England. ✓

Write It!

Ask the students to write the opposite of each word you say. Use the following words: *happy (sad), new (old), night (day), high (low), in front (behind), many (few), above (below).*

Little Book: *Go, Pete!*

Key Words: Pete, green, team, new, he, use, blue, see, hear, Sue, clear, sleep, Rose, eat, behind, blow, tree, low, slow, float, near, feet, go, goes, huge, home, don't, field

Phonics Objectives

Can students:
✓ listen for the long *o, e,* and *u* sounds?
✓ read words with the long vowels *o, e,* and *u* in the context of a story?
✓ write words with the long vowels *o, e, u?*

Language Acquisition Objectives

Can students:
✓ read words in story context?

ESL Standards

• Goal 3, Standard 2

The ball lands behind the fence right beside Rose.

The umpire yells, "Home run!"

"Don't let Rose get the ball!" cries Mike.

But no ball is in the grass.

Rose likes home runs.

8

A low, slow ball floats near his feet.

Pete lets it go. He taps his bat and waits.

The next ball is a fast ball.

He steps up. He hits it.

The ball goes back… back… back to the trees.

It's a huge hit! The green team cries, "Go, Pete!"

6

1

3

DEVELOPING PHONEMIC AWARENESS

Invite students to listen as you recite (or play) the cheer below. Ask them to listen to the long vowel sounds /ō/, /ē/, and /ü/.

> Pete, Pete
> hit the ball!
> Hit the ball
> to the wall!
>
> Sue, Sue
> go, go, go!
> Swing that bat
> high and low!

Invite children to recite the cheer with you. Then ask for volunteers to perform the cheer like they are cheerleaders at a baseball game.

USING THE LITTLE BOOK

Explain to the students that they are going to make a Little Book about a baseball game. Ask them to remove pages 57 and 58 from their books. Show them how to cut the page on the dotted line with the scissors icon, then fold the pages to make their own eight-page Little Book.

Preview *Go, Pete!* by reading the title aloud to the class. Allow the students time to look through the book and examine the pictures. Ask the students to follow along and track the words in the Little Book as you read the story aloud to them.

Engage the class in the story. Draw upon students' experiences and feelings about the story to spark their interest. Ask students who are familiar with baseball to explain the rules of the game to the others. Ask them questions such as *Do you ever play baseball? Did you ever lose a game? How did you feel?*

Revisit the story. Lead the class in a second reading of *Go, Pete!* This time, ask for volunteers to read aloud one page at a time. After each page is read, ask questions focusing on the content of the story. Here are some examples:

• *Who is batting?*
• *Why doesn't Pete swing at the first pitch?*
• *What are Gus and Rose doing?*
• *What happens to the ball?*
• *Why does Rose like home runs?*

INCLUDING ALL LEARNERS

Act Out the Story: *Go, Pete!*
(Kinesthetic/Auditory Learners)

Ask for four volunteers to act out the story *Go, Pete!* Assign the roles of Pete, Mike, Sue, Kate, and the umpire. If you want, you can also invite two other students to play the pets Rose the Goat and Gus the Dog.

Have the volunteers act out the story as you read it aloud to the class. Encourage the student playing Pete to mime hitting the ball with the imaginary bat. (Since there are a few lines of dialogue in the story, you may want to rehearse the spoken lines.)

When you are done, call on a new group of actors. Ask a volunteer to read the story aloud while the actors perform it. Encourage other groups of students to perform the story for the class.

Baseball Relay Game
(Kinesthetic/Visual Learners)

Materials: pictures of long *o*, *e*, and *u* words, four chairs

Set up four chairs around the room: three chairs at bases 1, 2, and 3 and the fourth chair at home plate. Divide the class into baseball teams. Then show the pictures. The first team to call out the correct word advances one base. One representative from each team moves from home plate to first, then second, then third base, and then back to home. Each time a team reaches home plate, it scores a point.

Story Time
(Extra Help)

Give students extra time to read the story quietly. Have students give summaries of what happened in the story. Ask them about their baseball heroes. Then encourage them to tell about a time when they played a game or a sport. Have students get into small groups and tell their stories.

Pete is on the green team.

He steps up to the plate and taps his bat.

It's a new bat, and he can't wait to use it.

The blue team is in the field.

Pete sees Kate and Mike.

He hears Sue say, "Go, Pete!"

2

7

The day is sunny and clear.

Gus sleeps by the bikes.

Rose eats grass behind the fence.

A little wind blows the trees.

It's a nice day for a baseball game.

Pete waits. He taps his bat on the plate.

4

5

Say It!

Read the story aloud again and have the students clap each time they hear you say words with the long *o*, *e*, and *u* sounds. ✓

Write It!

Challenge the students to look through their Little Book *Go, Pete!* and list all the names and words that have the long *o*, long *e*, and long *u* sounds in them. Ask students to write three sentences including words from their lists. When they are finished, review the activity as a class. ✓

Family Connection

Send home the Little Book *Go, Pete!* Encourage students to read the book to a family member.

BOOK CORNER

/ō/ o, o-e
The Adventures of Mole and Troll by Tony Johnson

/ō/ ow
The Snowy Day by Ezra Jack Keats

/ō/ oa, /ē/ ee
The Three Billy Goats Gruff by Paul Galdone

/ē/ ey
Pedro and the Monkey by Robert D. San Souci

/ü/ ew, ue
New Blue Shoes by Eve Rice

/ū/ u
The Troll Music by Anita Lobel

Review

Long Vowels: o, e, u

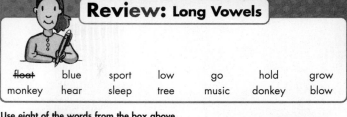

Review: Long Vowels

float	blue	sport	low	go	hold	grow
monkey	hear	sleep	tree	music	donkey	blow

Use eight of the words from the box above to finish the sentences.

1. A rowboat can ___float___ in a lake.

2. The wind can _____ in an open window.

3. A plant can _____ in the sun by a window.

4. Basketball is a _____ like baseball and tennis.

5. A _____ has green leaves.

6. A _____ is gray, has four legs and big ears, and eats grass.

7. A flute can make _____ .

8. The sky is clear and _____ on a nice day.

Review of Long Vowels: /ō/, /ē/, /ū/; Verbs; Adjectives   **Unit 6** **59**

DEVELOPING PHONEMIC AWARENESS

Place three chairs at the front of the class and ask for three volunteers to sit in them. Hand the first student a card with "LONG O" written on it, the second student a card with "LONG E" written on it, and the third student a card with "LONG U" written on it. Challenge each student to say a word with their long vowel sound in it. Instruct the children to listen carefully as you say a list of words. If they hear a word with their long vowel sound in it, they should pop up out of their chair. Use the following words: *blue, sleep, grow, low, fruit, read, feet, flute, clear, juice, me.* Continue with other students. You can extend the activity by adding words that have no long vowel sounds.

USING THE REVIEW PAGE

Ask students to:
• locate the words as you say them
• read aloud and track words with you

Explain that they will be reviewing the long vowel sounds /ō/, /ē/, /ü/, and /ū/ on this page. Ask a volunteer to read aloud the long vowel words in the box. Invite another student to point out which words are adjectives and which are verbs.

INCLUDING ALL LEARNERS

Finish the Rhyme
(Auditory Learners)

Write *deer, float, cold, tree, blue* on the chalkboard. Read aloud the sentences below, stressing the underlined word. Then ask students to write the word on the board that completes each sentence and rhymes with the word you stress.

1. I <u>hear</u> a _____. *(deer)*
2. I <u>see</u> a _____. *(tree)*
3. Do <u>you</u> like _____. *(blue)*
4. I <u>know</u> my <u>boat</u> can _____. *(float)*
5. I'm <u>told</u> the wind is _____. *(cold)*

Say It!

 Teach the song "Oats, Peas, Beans." Preview unfamiliar words for students before teaching this song.

Oats, peas, beans and barley grow;
Oats, peas, beans and barley grow;
Do you or I or anyone know
How oats, peas, beans, and barley grow?

Ask students to identify words with the long o, e, and u sounds. ✓

Write It!

Ask the students to write four sentences of their own containing the long vowel words in the box at the top of the page. When they are finished, invite volunteers to read their sentences to the class. ✓

UNIT 7

Digraphs: sh, ph, th

Digraphs: /sh/ *sh*

Key Words: ship, sheep, shoe, wash, dish, fish, brush

Phonics Objectives

Can students:
✓ listen for and identify the /sh/ sound formed by the letter combination *sh?*
✓ read and write words and sentences with the /sh/ sound?

Students:
• distinguish between the /i/ in *ship* and the /ē/ in *sheep*

Language Acquisition Objectives

Can students:
✓ use the verb *wash?*

ESL Standards

• Goal 2, Standard 1

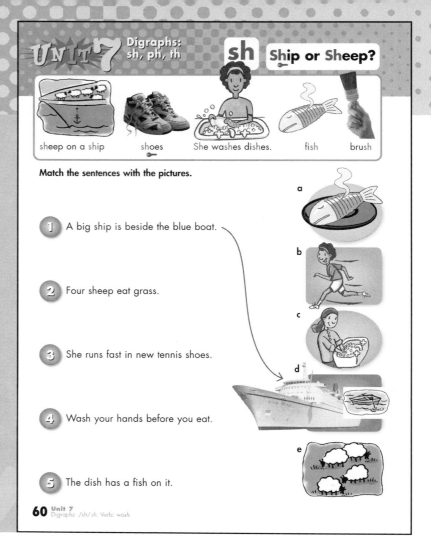

UNIT 7 Digraphs: sh, ph, th — sh — **Ship or Sheep?**

sheep on a ship | shoes | She washes dishes. | fish | brush

Match the sentences with the pictures.

1. A big ship is beside the blue boat.
2. Four sheep eat grass.
3. She runs fast in new tennis shoes.
4. Wash your hands before you eat.
5. The dish has a fish on it.

60 Unit 7
Digraphs /sh/ sh. Verb: wash

DEVELOPING PHONEMIC AWARENESS

Put your fingers to your lips and say *shhhhh* to indicate that you want the class to be quiet. Ask students to listen carefully as you say some words. Tell them to repeat each word and if it has the /sh/ sound in it, they should put their finger to their lips and say *shhhhh*. Point out that the /sh/ sound may be at the beginning, middle, or end of a word. You can use the following words: *ship, shoes, see, sheep, went, wash, fine, fish, bus, brush*. Ask students to practice blending /sh/ with the sounds of the other letters in the words.

USING PAGE 60

Ask students to:
• point to the letters *sh*
• locate the words as you say them
• read aloud and track words with you

Read the title of the page *Ship or Sheep?* aloud. Compare the /i/ sound in *ship* and the /ē/ sound in *sheep*. Point out how the *sh* letters stand for the /sh/ sound. Ask students to look at the sentence *She washes dishes,* read it aloud, and demonstrate the verb *wash*. Ask volunteers to create sentences of their own using the verb *wash*.

INCLUDING ALL LEARNERS

Fish for *sh* Words
(Kinesthetic/Visual Learners)

Materials: construction paper, markers or crayons, scissors, large paper bag

Distribute the materials. Ask students to cut out the shape of a fish and write one of the *sh* words from the page on it. When they are finished, ask students to drop their fish into a big paper bag. One at a time, invite students to "go fishing" by pulling a fish from the bag and reading the word on it aloud.

Say It!

Teach the class the following chant.

> I wish. I wish.
> I wish I could be a fish.
> A fish is what I wish to be.
> Swimming in the deep blue sea.
> I wish. I wish.
> I wish I could be a fish.

Ask students to clap every time they hear the /sh/ sound. ✓

Write It!

Write the words *ship, sheep, wash,* and *brush* on the chalkboard. Then read the following riddles to the class. After each riddle, ask students to write down the *sh* word answer.

1. You do this after you get dirty. *(wash)*
2. You use me on your hair. *(brush)*
3. You can sail on me. *(ship)*
4. You can find me on a farm. *(sheep)* ✓

ph On the Phone

telephone   earphones   elephant   graph   Phonics Team photo

Fill in the phone conversation. Write the words that finish each sentence.

Pete: Hi, Mike.

Mike: Hi, Pete.

Pete: Do you want to ___**play baseball**___ ?
                                                play baseball/ride an elephant

Mike: Sure, do you have your _____ ?
                                                          new earphones/new bat

Pete: Yes. Do you _____ ?
                                have a mitt/have a dish

Mike: Yes. Can Kate play _____ ?
                                            on the ship/on the team

Pete: Sure, _____ .
                        he can play/she can play

Mike: Okay, let's play on _____
                                            the big field/the big sheep

Pete: Okay. Bye, Mike.

Mike: Bye!

Digraphs: /f/ ph; Questions with do you...?   **Unit 7 61**

Digraphs: /f/ ph

Key Words: phone, telephone, earphones, elephant, graph, phonics, photo

Phonics Objectives

Can students:
- ✓ listen for the /f/ sound?
- ✓ identify the /f/ sound formed by the letter combination *ph?*
- ✓ read and write words and sentences with the /f/ sound?

Language Acquisition Objectives

Students:
- use questions beginning with *Do you . . .*

ESL Standards
- Goal 1, Standard 3
- Goal 3, Standard 2

BUILDING BACKGROUND

Bring in two telephones. Point to one and say *phone* aloud, stressing the /f/ sound. Ask students to repeat it with you. Ask the class if they enjoy talking on the telephone. Invite students to tell you how people say "Hello" on the phone in other countries.

Place the two telephones on your desk and invite two volunteers to have a phone conversation. Give the students a scenario such as "Student 1, the caller, wants to ask Student 2 if he can borrow her bicycle this weekend." Students may need scripts or cues to help them get started. Challenge the volunteers to improvise the conversation. When they are finished, invite other pairs to brainstorm other phone conversation topics and improvise these scenarios on the two telephones.

USING PAGE 61

Ask students to:
- point to the letters *ph*
- locate the words as you say them
- read aloud and track words with you

Point to the word *phone* in the title of the page and explain that, in English, the letters *ph* often stand for the same sound as the letter *f*. Say the /f/ sound. Tell students that the /f/ sound can be at the beginning, middle, or end of words and ask students to point out examples on the page.

INCLUDING ALL LEARNERS

Write Phone Dialogues
(Auditory Learners)

Tell students to think of things they might talk about on the phone. Write a list of their ideas on the chalkboard. Then invite them to write their own phone dialogues about a topic they choose. Volunteers can read their phone dialogues or act them out with a partner for the class.

Say It!

 Teach your class the following chant.

Phonics are . . . Phonics are . . .
Phonics are fun!
Phonics are fun for everyone.
Phonics are . . . Phonics are . . .
Phonics are cool!
Fee, fie, phonics
Phonics are fun in school!

After students are comfortable with the chant, invite pairs to recite it to the rest of the class in unison. ✓

Write It!

 Make a hand-out for the class listing misspellings with the correct spelling for the following words: *elephant, graph, phone, earphones, phonics, photo, telephone.* For example, list *elefant, elephant, elaphunt.* Include misspellings with *f* in place of *ph.* Ask students to circle the correct one. Review the work as a class. ✓

Digraphs: /th/ *th* (voiceless)

Key Words: thick, thin, thumb, throw, bath, think, math, three, month

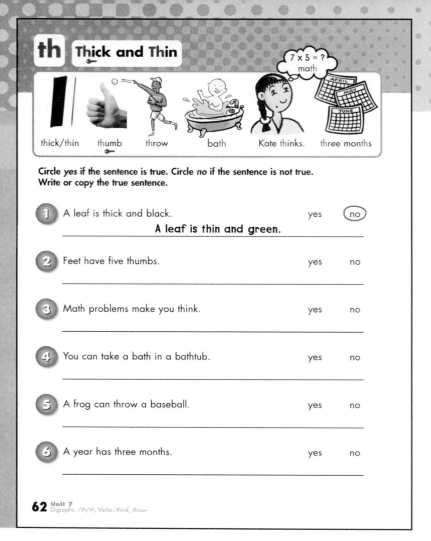

th Thick and Thin

thick/thin   thumb   throw   bath   Kate thinks.   three months

7 × 5 = ?
math

**Circle *yes* if the sentence is true. Circle *no* if the sentence is not true.
Write or copy the true sentence.**

1. A leaf is thick and black.   yes   (no)
   A leaf is thin and green.

2. Feet have five thumbs.   yes   no

3. Math problems make you think.   yes   no

4. You can take a bath in a bathtub.   yes   no

5. A frog can throw a baseball.   yes   no

6. A year has three months.   yes   no

62 Unit 7
Digraphs: /th/ *th*, Verbs: *think, throw*

Phonics Objectives

Can students:
- ✓ listen for the /th/ sound?
- ✓ identify the /th/ sound formed by the letter combination *th*?
- ✓ read and write words and sentences with the /th/ sound?

Language Acquisition Objectives

Can students:
- ✓ use the verbs *think* and *throw*?

ESL Standards

- Goal 2, Standard 2

DEVELOPING PHONEMIC AWARENESS

Hold up your thumb and say the word *thumb,* stressing the /th/ sound. Invite students to say the word and hold up their own thumbs. Say the word *thumbs* slowly and model blending the /th/ with the sounds of the other letters: *thuuuummmbsss.*

Ask the class to listen carefully as you say some words with the /th/ sound. Tell them to repeat each word. If the word has the /th/ sound at the beginning, they should hold up their thumb. If the word has the /th/ sound at the end, they should hold up their little finger. Use the following words: *thick, thin, bath, throw, thumb, math, month, three.*

USING PAGE 62

Ask students to:
- point to the letters *th*
- locate the words as you say them
- read aloud and track words with you

Point out *three months* on the page and display three months in a calendar. Read aloud the days of the week on the calendar and point out that *Thursday* begins with the /th/ sound. Then show how the third, thirteenth, and thirtieth days of a month begin with the /th/ sound. Make a birthday calendar highlighting students' birthdays.

INCLUDING ALL LEARNERS

Throw a *th* Word
(Kinesthetic Learners)

Materials: a small soft toy or ball of yarn

Write the *th* words on the chalkboard. Take the toy or ball of yarn and toss it to a student. Ask that student to say one of the words on the board, then toss the toy to another student who must do the same. Continue until all students have caught the toy and said a *th* word.

Say It!

 Teach the class the following rhyme.

My thumb points up.
My thumb points down.
My thumb is thick and short and round.
It may sound silly,
It may sound dumb.
But how could I _____ without my thumb?

Ask students to come up with verbs such as *eat, write,* or *throw* to fill in the blank. ✓

Write It!

Write *thick, throw, think,* and *month* on the chalkboard. Preview new vocabulary and read aloud the following incomplete sentences. Ask students to write the *th* word that fits each blank.

1. _____ the ball and I will catch it. *(throw)*
2. You can skate on _____ ice. *(thick)*
3. Math makes me _____ . *(think)*
4. My favorite _____ is June. *(month)* ✓

th **Fun with the Phonics Team**

Bob and Gus dash.

thump

Kate shakes the mat.

splash

Write the word that finishes each sentence.

1. Tim plays ball with ___**Mike**___ and lands with a thump.

2. Nan is in the rowboat with _____ and hears a splash.

3. Gus dashes on the sand with _____.

4. Sue sits with _____ and plays the flute.

5. Tab is in the grass with _____.

6. Kate shakes a mat near Pete and _____.

Unit 7 63
Digraphs: /th /th: Preposition: *with*

Digraphs: /th/ *th*
(voiceless)
Key Word: with

Phonics Objectives

Can students:
✓ listen for the /th/ sound?
✓ identify the /th/ sound formed by the letter combination *th?*
✓ read and write words and sentences with the /th/ sound?

Language Acquisition Objectives

Can students:
✓ use the preposition *with?*

Students:
• review prepositions *in, on, near*

ESL Standards

• Goal 2, Standard 2

BUILDING BACKGROUND

Say the word *with,* stressing the /th/ sound, and ask students to repeat it after you. Tell students that when you use *with* for people or things, it means the people or things are together. Ask a volunteer to stand next to you and say, *(student's name) is with me.* Ask students to get into pairs and say who they are *with.* Then give directions to students using the word *with,* such as *Go with (student's name) to the board.* Discuss with students other ways they can use *with* in phrases such as *coffee with milk* or a *class with desks.* Explain that in these cases, *with* means "has."

USING PAGE 63

Ask students to:
• point to the letters *th*
• locate the words as you say them
• read aloud and track words with you

Go over the scene on the page with the class. *Who is in the scene? What is happening? What noises are there?* Read the title, *Fun with the Phonics Team,* and point out the /th/ sound of the letters *th* in the word *with.* Then talk about the ways you use *with* in conversation, such as *chant* with *me* or *walk* with *me.*

INCLUDING ALL LEARNERS

The "With" Game
(Visual Learners)

Materials: magazine pictures of different people

Display an assortment of pictures on the chalk rail. Then say sentences using the word *with,* such as *Point to the girl with the dog* or *Point to the boy with the bicycle.* Call on students to point to the person you describe.

Say It!

 Divide the class into two groups, A and B. Then have them recite this dialogue:

A: What's this? (show a Picture Card or picture)
B: A dog.
A: Say it with me again.
A + B: A dog!

Encourage students to follow the same pattern using different pictures and switching roles. ✓

Write It!

Dictate the following sentences using the word *with.*

1. Tim plays with Nan.
2. Gus is with Rose.
3. Tab runs with Kate.
4. Dan is in the boat with Gus.

When students are finished, review the sentences as a class. ✓

Digraphs: /<u>th</u>/ *th* (voiced)

Key Words: this, that

Phonics Objectives

Can students:
- ✓ listen for the /<u>th</u>/ sound?
- ✓ identify the /<u>th</u>/ sound formed by the letter combination *th?*
- ✓ read and write words and sentences with the /<u>th</u>/ sound?

Language Acquisition Objectives

Students:
- use rhyming words
- use the demonstrative pronouns and adjectives *this* and *that*

ESL Standards

- Goal 2, Standard 3

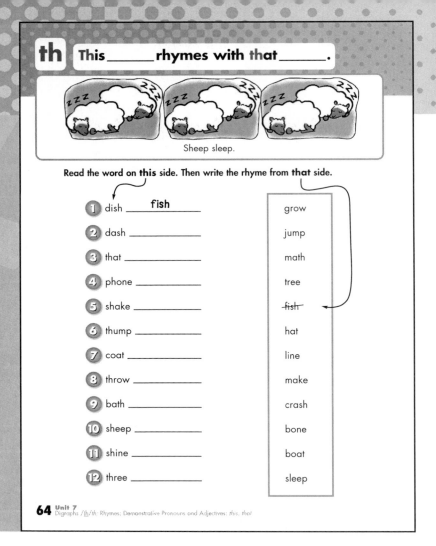

DEVELOPING PHONEMIC AWARENESS

Say the words *this* and *thick*, stressing the /<u>th</u>/ and /th/ sounds. *Do you hear a difference in the sounds at the beginning of the words?* Point out that both words begin with the same *th* letters, but the letters make two different sounds. Compare the voiced /<u>th</u>/ sound in *this* with the unvoiced /th/ sound in *thick.* Explain that to make the /<u>th</u>/ sound, you place your tongue tip between your teeth before pronouncing the sound. Model for the class how to make the /<u>th</u>/ sound, blend this sound into words, and let students practice saying *this* and *that.*

USING PAGE 64

Ask students to:
- point to the letters *th*
- locate the words as you say them
- read aloud and track words with you

Read aloud the title of the page, *This . . . rhymes with that . . .* stressing the /<u>th</u>/sound. Explain that we say *this* for things that are near and *that* for things that are far away. Hold up a pen. *This is a pen.* Then point to the window. *That is a window.* Ask volunteers to make up *This is . . . / That is . . .* sentences using something close for *this* and something far for *that.* Explain that *this* and *that* are both demonstrative pronouns and adjectives. When used alone they are pronouns, but when they describe something they are adjectives. Point out how *this* and *that* are used on the page.

INCLUDING ALL LEARNERS

This and That Grab Bag
(Kinesthetic/Visual Learners)

Materials: assorted objects, large bag

Place some small, familiar objects in a bag. Ask a volunteer to take two objects from the bag, place one on a desk, and hold the other. Let the student say, *This is a (object in hand),* and then point to the object on the desk and say, *That is a (object on desk).*

Say It!

 Teach the class the following rhyme.

> Look at this shirt.
> Look at that dress.
> Yikes! I have never seen such a mess.
> Pick up a mop.
> Then pick up a broom.
> I think it's time to clean up this room!

Recite the rhyme as a class. Then invite volunteers to recite it. ✔

Write It!

 Write the following words on the chalkboard: *this, thump, bath, that, math, then.* Then read the words to the class, stressing the /th/ and /<u>th</u>/ sounds. Ask students to write down the words that have the voiced /<u>th</u>/ sound. ✔

Little Book: *The Bath*

Key Words: splash, shake, bathtub, three, then, wash, with, dash, thick, bathtub, phone, fish, thump

Phonics Objectives
Can students:
✓ listen for the digraph sounds /sh/, /ph/, and /th/?
✓ read words with the digraphs *sh*, *ph*, and *th* in the context of a story?
✓ write words with *sh*, *ph*, *th*?

Language Acquisition Objectives
Can students:
✓ read words in story context?

Students:
• use the preposition *with*

ESL Standards
• Goal 1, Standard 2

Bob is on the phone and can't stop Gus.

Gus dashes by like a wet fish.

The back door is open, and he races onto the grass.

Bob hears: Thump!

SHAKE, SHAKE, SHAKE! Thump!

Then Bob hears the phone.

"Oh, no!" he says. "Sit, Gus. Stay!"

But Gus jumps onto the floor with a splash.

He slips on the wet floor.

SHAKE, SHAKE, SHAKE!

The brushes crash.

Gus dashes for the door.

DEVELOPING PHONEMIC AWARENESS

To warm students up for the story *The Bath*, teach them the following chant.

> Gus needs a bath.
> A bath, bath, bath.
> Put him in the tub.
> The tub, tub, tub.
> Take a brush and rub.
> Rub, rub, rub!

Invite volunteers to model blending the sounds in words from the chant. For example, ask a student to say the word *brush* and demonstrate blending the sounds /br/, /u/, and /sh/ together.

Tell students that in *The Bath* they will find out what happens when Bob tries to give Gus the dog a bath. Ask if anyone in the class has a dog. *Do you ever give your dog a bath? How? What happens?*

USING THE LITTLE BOOK

Explain to students that they are going to make a Little Book about Bob and Gus the dog. Ask them to remove pages 65 and 66 from their books. Show them how to cut the page on the dotted line with the scissors icon, then fold the pages to make their own eight-page Little Book.

Preview *The Bath* by reading the title aloud to the class. Allow students time to look through the book and examine the pictures. Ask students to follow along and track the words in the Little Book as you read the story aloud to them.

Engage the class in the story. Draw upon students' experiences and feelings about the story to spark their interest. Ask them questions such as *Do you like to take baths? Did you ever try to give a pet a bath? Did you ever spill something and get a room all wet?*

Revisit the story. Lead the class in a second reading of *The Bath*. This time, ask for volunteers to read aloud one page at a time. After each page is read, ask questions focusing on the content of the story. Here are some examples:

• *Why is Gus unhappy?*
• *How does Gus get out of the tub?*
• *What happens to the bathroom?*
• *Who gets wet?*

Including All Learners

Act Out the Story: *The Bath*
(Kinesthetic/Auditory Learners)

Ask for two volunteers to act out the story *The Bath*. Assign the roles of Bob and Gus the dog. Let volunteers act out the story as you read it to the class. Instruct the student playing Bob to pretend to wash Gus's back. You may wish to pause at speech balloons and let students read them aloud.

When you are done, invite a new group of students to act out the story. This time, ask other students to take turns reading pages of the story while the actors perform it.

Change the Story
(Auditory Learners)

Materials: chart paper, marker

Brainstorm with students a new ending or new parts to the story. To get them started, tell them to imagine what would happen if Bob brought Gus back in for another try, if he decided to wash the cat, or if the phone didn't ring. Guide students, writing down appropriate suggestions that make for an interesting new ending or new parts to the story. When you are finished, read the new story aloud.

Story Time
(Extra Help)

Give students extra time to read the story aloud to each other. Ask students to give summaries of what happens in the story. Then encourage them to tell about a time when they got splashed or wet or made a mess when trying to help. Invite students to form small groups and share their stories.

Splash! Splash!

SHAKE! SHAKE! SHAKE!

Gus is in the bathtub.

He splashes and shakes three more times.

Bob takes the soap and washes his back.

Then he washes all the soap off.

He holds on to Gus with his hand.

❷   ❼

Gus is not happy

His thick coat is wet and cold.

He wants to jump from the bathtub.

But Bob holds him back and washes his ears.

Gus goes SHAKE, SHAKE, SHAKE.

Bob gets wet, and the floor gets wet.

❹   ❺

Say It!

Give students time to read the story aloud. Then engage the class in a discussion about words they read in the story. *Which words have the /sh/ sound? The /th/ sound? The /th/ sound? The /f/ sound?* ✓

Write It!

Challenge students to look through their Little Book *The Bath* and copy down all the words that have the /sh/, /th/, /th/, and /f/ sounds in them. When they are finished, review the activity as a class. ✓

Family Connection

Send home the Little Book *The Bath*. Encourage students to read the book to a family member.

BOOK CORNER

/sh/ sh
Sheila Rae, the Brave by Kevin Henkes

/f/ ph
Nate the Great and the Phony Clue by Marjorie Weinman Sharmat

/th/ th
Thunder Cake by Patricia Polacco

/th/ th
This and That by Julie Sykes

/th/ th, /th/ th
There's an Ant in Anthony by Bernard Most

Digraphs: *sh, ph, th*

Review: These Clothes, Those Clothes

These shoes are blue.

Those shoes are red.

Which of **these** clothes go with **those** clothes?
Match the clothes that are the same colors and write the answers.

those green shoes	those blue shoes
that black hat	~~those tan socks~~
those red shoes	that red and blue cap
that yellow rain hat	

1. these tan pants ___those tan socks___
2. these blue socks _____
3. this yellow raincoat _____
4. this green dress _____
5. this red and blue jacket _____
6. this black coat _____
7. these red shorts _____

Review of Digraphs: /sh/sh, /th/th; Demonstrative Pronouns and Adjectives: these, those

Unit 7 **67**

Phonics Objectives

Can students:
- ✓ listen for and identify the /sh/ and /th/ sounds formed by letter combinations *sh* and *th*?
- ✓ read and write words with the /sh/ and /th/ sounds?

Language Acquisition Objectives

Can students:
- ✓ use the demonstrative pronouns and adjectives *these* and *those*?
- ✓ use singular and plurals?

ESL Standards
- Goal 2, Standard 2

BUILDING BACKGROUND

Place three pencils on your desk and move away from the desk. Hold up three pens in your hand. Say, *These are pens.* Then point to the pencils at a distance on the desk and say, *Those are pencils.* Hand the three pens to a student and ask him or her to say, *These are pens.* Then ask the student to point to the pencils and say, *Those are pencils.* Ask volunteers to make up *These are . . . / Those are . . .* sentences of their own.

Write *this* and *that* on the chalkboard. Explain that these demonstrative pronouns are used when talking about one thing. Write *these* and *those* on the chalkboard and explain that these demonstrative pronouns are used when talking about more than one thing. Point out that *this, that, these,* and *those* also function as adjectives.

USING THE REVIEW PAGE

Ask students to:
- point to the letters *th*
- locate the words as you say them
- read aloud and track words with you

Read the title of the page aloud. Explain how *these* and *those* are used in the box. Point out that *th* is not pronounced in the word *clothes.* Discuss the clothes students are wearing and review colors. Then explain that they will match clothes that are the same color using *this, that, these,* and *those* as adjectives.

INCLUDING ALL LEARNERS

This and These Grab Bag
(Kinesthetic/Auditory Learners)

Materials: a large bag, pictures

Locate pictures of single items and multiple items, such as one car or two buses. Place the pictures in a bag. Ask a volunteer to pull a picture out of the bag and say, *This is a (item in picture)* or *These are (items in picture).* Continue with more volunteers.

Say It!

Teach this rhyme.

This is my right foot.
Those are my toes.
These are my ears.
And this is my nose.

Students can point to body parts as they recite the rhyme. ✔

Write It!

Write *this* and *these* on the chalkboard. Then write the following sentences with blanks on the chalkboard. Read each sentence aloud, and then ask students to write down the sentence, filling the blank with *this* or *these.*

1. Do you want _____ apple? *(this)*
2. I found _____ coins. *(these)*
3. I read _____ book. *(this)*
4. _____ plants are dry. *(These)* ✔

UNIT 8

Digraphs: wh, ng, ch, tch, wr, kn

Digraphs: /hw/ wh

Key Words: what, white, whale, wheel, whistle, wheat

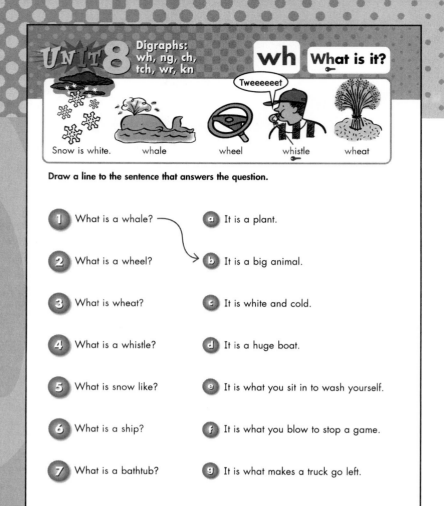

UNIT 8 Digraphs: wh, ng, ch, tch, wr, kn

wh What is it?

Snow is white.   whale   wheel   whistle   wheat

Tweeeeeet

Draw a line to the sentence that answers the question.

1. What is a whale? — a. It is a plant.
2. What is a wheel? — b. It is a big animal.
3. What is wheat? — c. It is white and cold.
4. What is a whistle? — d. It is a huge boat.
5. What is snow like? — e. It is what you sit in to wash yourself.
6. What is a ship? — f. It is what you blow to stop a game.
7. What is a bathtub? — g. It is what makes a truck go left.

68 Unit 8
Digraphs: /hw/ wh, Questions with *what?*

Phonics Objectives

Can students:
✓ listen for the /hw/ sound?
✓ identify the /hw/ sound formed by the letter combination *wh*?
✓ read and write words and sentences with the /hw/ sound?

Language Acquisition Objectives

Can students:
✓ use the question word *what?*

ESL Standards

• Goal 2, Standard 1

DEVELOPING PHONEMIC AWARENESS

Ask students to hold a finger in front of their mouths as they repeat the following words after you: *white, whale, wheel, whistle, wheat.* Ask, *Do you feel your breath blow on your finger?* Then ask students to keep their fingers in place and repeat these words after you: *wet, window, water, wind, wash.* Ask again, *Do you feel your breath blow on your finger?* Explain that the first set of words begins with the letters *wh*, which stand for the /hw/ sound. The /h/ sound comes right before the /w/ sound and makes their breath blow on their finger when they make the /hw/ sound. Invite students to practice forming this sound.

Say *whistle* and whistle or blow a whistle. Ask students to listen as you say the following words, repeat each word, and whistle if it begins with the /hw/ sound: *white, wet, water, what, wheat, window, whale, wheel, wash, wind.*

USING PAGE 68

Ask students to:
• point to the letters *wh*
• locate the words as you say them
• read aloud and track words with you

Read aloud the title of the page, *What is it?*, stressing the /hw/ sound. Explain that many questions begin with *what.* Then explain that there are five question words in English that start with the letters *wh* and make the /hw/ sound: *what, where, when, why, who.* Give example questions beginning with these words and ask students to brainstorm some questions.

INCLUDING ALL LEARNERS

What Is It?
(Kinesthetic/Visual Learners)

Materials: pictures of common items, bag

Place an assortment of pictures in a bag. Ask a volunteer to play the "teacher," draw a picture from the bag, and peek at it.

Ask a second student to ask, *What is it?* The first student gives clues about the picture. The second student guesses what it is. Then the second student picks a picture and plays "teacher."

Say It!

 Teach the following chant.

What, what, what is that?
What is that I see?
It's not a whale.
It's not a wheel.
It's a _____ by a tree.

Ask students to come up with different words to fill in the blank. ✓

Write It!

Write *white, whale, whistle,* and *wheat* on the chalkboard. Read the following riddles and ask students to write the *wh* word answer after each riddle.

1. You can make a noise with me. *(whistle)*
2. I am the color of snow. *(white)*
3. I am a plant you can eat. *(wheat)*
4. I am the biggest animal. *(whale)*

Digraphs: /hw/ wh

Key Words: when, one, two, three, four, five, six, seven, eight, nine, ten, eleven, twelve

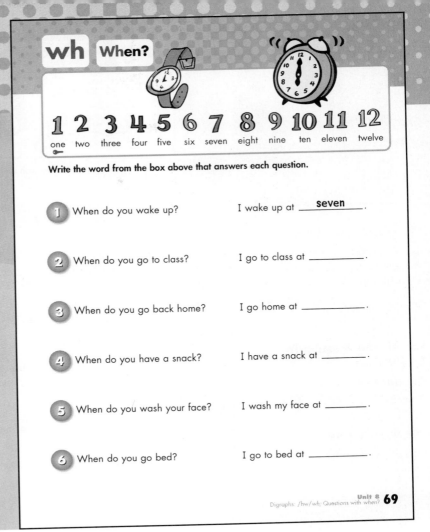

Phonics Objectives

Can students:
- ✓ listen for the /hw/ sound?
- ✓ identify the /hw/ sound formed by the letter combination *wh*?
- ✓ read and write words and sentences with the /hw/ sound?

Language Acquisition Objectives

Can students:
- ✓ use the question word *when?*
- ✓ use the numbers 1–12?
- ✓ tell time using the numbers 1–12?

ESL Standards

- Goal 1, Standard 2

DEVELOPING PHONEMIC AWARENESS

Say *when* for the class, stressing the initial /hw/ sound. Ask the class to repeat it. Model again how the sound is formed by saying the /h/ and then the /w/ sound. Then explain that the word *when* is used to ask questions about time.

Display a time teaching clock. Ask students, *When do you wake up?* Invite a volunteer to position the hands on the clock to show the time he or she wakes up. Ask other *when* questions, inviting students to answer by positioning the hands on the clock. *When does school end? When do you eat lunch? When do you go to sleep?*

USING PAGE 69

Ask students to:

- point to the letters *wh*
- locate the words as you say them
- read aloud and track words with you

Point out the title of the page, *When?* and explain that students will learn about numbers and telling time on this page. Teach the numbers in the box. Then show various hours on the clock and read them aloud. Contrast this kind of clock with a twenty-four-hour clock used in other countries. Explain that the day is divided into two sets of twelve hours each. A.M. refers to the twelve hours from midnight to noon. P.M. refers to the twelve hours from noon until midnight.

INCLUDING ALL LEARNERS

Make a Clock
(Kinesthetic/Visual Learners)

Materials: white paper plates, tag board, scissors, brass fasteners, markers

Distribute the materials. Ask students to write the numerals 1–12 around the paper plates to make clocks. Let students cut clock hands out of the tag board and then show them how to fasten the hands to the face with the brass fastener. Ask

when questions and let students answer by positioning their clock's hands.

Say It!

 Teach the following rhyme. 🎧

When do you feel fine?
I feel fine at nine!
When do you feel great?
I feel great at eight.
When do you have fun?
I have fun at one!

Teach the rhyme two lines at a time. Let students come up with additional rhymes. ✓

Write It!

Dictate the following questions. Ask students to write each question, followed by a sentence answer. Some students may need to refer to their Student Book to check their spelling.

1. When do you get up?
2. When do you go to sleep?
3. When do you have fun?
4. When do you go to class? ✓

Digraphs: /ng/ *ng*

Key Words: sing, song, king, ring, long, string, swing

ng Sing a song.

Sue sings a song.   The king has a ring.   a long string   swing

Write the word that finishes each sentence.

1. Sue sings a ___**song**___ .
   string/song

2. The kite has a long _____ .
   string/swing

3. The _____ hangs from the tree.
   song/swing

4. The _____ has a big ring.
   king/string

5. Nan can make the _____ go high.
   swing/ring

6. A snake is _____ , like a stick.
   song/long

70 Unit 8
Digraphs: /ng/ng; Verb: sing

DEVELOPING PHONEMIC AWARENESS

Bring a bell into class. Ring the bell for the students, and then say the word *ring*, stressing the /ng/ sound. Ask students to say it with you. Explain that some words in English end with the same sound as *ring* and *song*. Show students how to make this sound by lifting the back of the tongue to the roof of their mouths. This is a nasal sound that students may not know. Let them practice making the /ng/ sound a few times.

Hand the bell to a volunteer. Ask the student to listen carefully as you say some words. Ask the student to ring the bell every time he or she hears a word that ends with the same sound as *ring* and *song*. Use the following words: *sun, song, king, can, swing, swim, line, long, stand, string.* Allow other students to take the bell and listen for /ng/ words.

USING PAGE 70

Ask students to:
- point to the letters *ng*
- locate the words as you say them
- read aloud and track words with you

Read aloud the title of the page, *Sing a song,* stressing the /ng/ sounds. Explain that *sing* is an action word and demonstrate by singing *la, la, la.* Tell students that you sing *songs.* Review songs that the students know and ask students about their favorites.

INCLUDING ALL LEARNERS

Songs We Sing
(Auditory Learners)

Divide the class into pairs or small groups. Invite them to rehearse a song and then sing it to the rest of the class. On a bulletin board, make a list titled *Songs We Sing* and list the titles of the songs the students selected.

Say It!

Teach the following chant.

The King and Queen can't sing a thing.
They scream and cry big tears.
The song they sing just comes out wrong.
You have to hold your ears!

Ask students to identify words with the /ng/ sound. ✓

Write It!

Write *swing, string, ring,* and *song* on the chalkboard. Read the following incomplete rhymes and ask students to write the word that completes each.

1. You can't go wrong if you sing a _____. (*song*)
2. The hand of the king has a gold ____. (*ring*)
3. My favorite thing is to play on a _____. (*swing*)
4. I can keep my ring if I tie it with _____. (*string*)

Review the answers as a class. ✓

Digraphs: /ng/ -ing

Key Word: thinking

-ing **Nan is thinking.**

$7 \times 5 = ?$

She is thinking. = She thinks.

Write the letter of the picture that matches the sentence on the line.

1. Sue is singing a song. __h__
2. Pete is reading. _____
3. Bev is washing the dishes. _____
4. Tim is swimming. _____
5. Mike is riding a bike. _____
6. Pete is sleeping. _____
7. Gus is eating the meat. _____
8. The frog is jumping. _____

Digraphs: /ng/ng; Present Progressive Verbs **Unit 8 71**

Phonics Objectives

Can students:
- ✓ listen for the final /ng/ sound?
- ✓ identify the /ng/ sound formed by the letter combination -ing?
- ✓ read and write words and sentences with the /ng/ sound?

Language Acquisition Objectives

Can students:
- ✓ use present progressive verbs (verb + -ing)

ESL Standards
- Goal 2, Standard 2

BUILDING BACKGROUND

On the chalkboard, write the word *think* and read it aloud. *What kind of word is* think? *(an action word, a verb)* Add -ing to *think,* forming the word *thinking.* Explain that the ending -ing can be added to action words to show that the action is happening right now. It is important to stress that *thinking* means that the action *think* is happening now, whereas *think* means the action *think* in general, at any time. The present progressive tense may be a new concept for some students.

Ask the class to listen as you say these action words and repeat each word with an -ing ending: *think, sing, wash, jump, read, sleep, eat.*

USING PAGE 71

Ask students to:
- point to the letters *ing*
- locate the words as you say them
- read aloud and track words with you

Read aloud the two sentences that are shown as "equal" in the box on the page. Explain that *thinking* refers to the action happening now. Then point out that some action words change before the -ing ending is added. Write *swim* and *swimming* on the chalkboard. Point out that an extra *m* was added before -ing. Write the words *ride* and *riding* on the chalkboard and explain how the final *e* in *ride* was dropped before -ing was added. Let students practice changing the endings of the words *take, make, run, hit,* and *jog* as they make them into -ing words.

INCLUDING ALL LEARNERS

Mime Actions
(Kinesthetic Learners)

Ask students to mime things that they are doing right now. Write their actions on the chalkboard and point out the -ing endings.

Then invite students to play charades in teams using action words.

Say It!

 Divide the class into groups A and B and teach the class the following rhyme.

A: Birds can sing.
B: They are singing.
A: Bells can ring.
B: They are ringing.
A: Bugs can creep.
B: They are creeping.
A: I can sleep.
B: Shhhhh! I'm sleeping.

Invite students to come up with additional lines in the same pattern. ✓

Write It!

 Ask the class to listen as you say some action words and to write the words with -ing endings: *wash, eat, read, jump, sleep, sing.* Review the work as a class. ✓

Digraphs: /ch/ *ch*

Key Words: cheese, lunch, sandwich, lunchbox, chicken, peach, chalk

ch Cheese for Lunch

cheese   sandwich   lunchbox   chicken   peach   chalk

Write the word that finishes each sentence.

1. Pete has cheese in his ___**sandwich**___.

2. The sandwich is in Pete's _____.

3. Kate is eating a _____.

4. The box of white _____ is on the desk.

5. Tab sees a _____ by the tree.

DEVELOPING PHONEMIC AWARENESS

Hold up a piece of chalk and say the word *chalk*. Point out that the letters *ch* work together to stand for the /ch/ sound. Show students how to form this sound by pushing out your lips slightly, putting your teeth together, and pushing the air out with your tongue as you say the /ch/ sound. Let students mimic your actions. Say *chalk* again and invite the class to repeat it after you. Then ask each student to repeat it to assess them individually. Invite volunteers to model blending the /ch/ with the sounds of other letters in words they know.

Ask students to listen as you say some words with the /ch/ sound, repeat each word, then tell you if the /ch/ sound is heard at the beginning, middle, or end of the word. You can use the following words: *cheese, peach, sandwich, lunchbox, chalk, chicken, lunch.*

USING PAGE 72

Ask students to:
• point to the letters *ch*
• locate the words as you say them
• read aloud and track words with you

Point out the words *cheese, sandwich, chicken,* and *peach* on the page and read them aloud. Ask what these words have in common besides the /ch/ sound. (*They are things that you can eat.*) Ask students to think of other foods with the /ch/ sound, such as *chips, chili, cheeseburgers.*

INCLUDING ALL LEARNERS

Make Menus
(**Visual Learners**)

Materials: drawing paper and markers or computer clip art

Divide the class into pairs or small groups. Distribute the materials and ask them to make menus, including at least three *ch* words. Encourage them to illustrate their menus first with their drawings or computer clip art and then label their drawings with words. Invite students to show their menus to the rest of the class.

Say It!

 Teach the following chant.

A chicken wing, an onion ring,
A slice of cheese to munch.
A peach or two, a bowl of stew,
Now that's a tasty lunch!

Recite the chant as a group. Ask students to clap every time they say the word with the /ch/ sound. ✓

Write It!

Ask students to write the following words: *cheese, lunch, chicken, peach, chalk, sandwich.* Tell them to circle the letters *ch* in each word. ✓

Digraphs: /ch/ tch

Key Words: catch, pitch, watch, scratch, match

tch | **Catch that pitch!**

Tim can catch a fast pitch.   Bob watches his watch.   scratch   match

Write the word that finishes each sentence.

1 Tim likes to catch, and Pete likes to ___**pitch**___ .

2 Bob has a _____ that says three o'clock.

3 Kate has a _____ on her hand.

4 Nan says, "Don't play with that _____!"

5 Mike likes to _____ baseball games on TV.

Digraphs: /ch/tch; Verbs: catch, watch, pitch   Unit 8 **73**

Phonics Objectives

Can students:
- ✓ listen for the /ch/ sound?
- ✓ identify the /ch/ sound formed by the letter combination *tch?*
- ✓ read and write words and sentences with the /ch/ sound *(tch)?*

Language Acquisition Objectives

Can students:
- ✓ use the verbs *catch, watch,* and *pitch?*
- ✓ use sports and baseball words?

ESL Standards
- • Goal 2, Standard 2

DEVELOPING PHONEMIC AWARENESS

Ask the class if anyone likes to play baseball. Say *pitch* and have the class repeat it. Do the same with *catch.* Ask, *What do both words have in common? (the /ch/ sound, the letters* tch) Explain that in English, the letters *tch* stand for the /ch/ sound. Say the word *catch* and model oral blending: *caaaaatch.* Remind them that the letters *ch* also stand for the /ch/ sound as in the word *lunch.*

Ask the class to imagine they are pitchers in a baseball game. Tell them to listen carefully as you say some words. They should repeat each word and, if the word has the /ch/ sound, they should make believe they are pitching a baseball. Use the following words: *cat, catch, sky, scratch, mats, match, watch, walk.*

USING PAGE 73

Ask students to:
- • point to the letters *tch*
- • locate the words as you say them
- • read aloud and track words with you

Explain that the word *watch* can be either an action word (verb) or noun. To illustrate this, point out the sentence on the page: *Bob watches his watch.* Read the sentence aloud to the class, and ask which *watch* is an action word and which *watch* is a noun. Point out that *pitch* and *catch* are also nouns and verbs. Let students brainstorm other words that function as both a noun and a verb.

INCLUDING ALL LEARNERS

Things I Watch on TV
(Visual Learners)

Materials: markers, drawing paper

Write *Things I Watch on TV* on the chalkboard and read it for the class. Let stu-

dents brainstorm things that they like to watch. Write their suggestions on the chalkboard. Distribute the drawing materials and ask the students to draw something in a TV screen and write a caption under it.

Say It!
Teach the following rhyme.

Watch Nan pitch.
Watch Nan catch.
Watch her throw the ball.
Watch her swing.
Watch her run.
She's the best of all!

Invite students to substitute students' names for Nan and change *her* to *him* for boys. ✓

Write It!
Ask students to write the following words as you read them: *pitch, catch, watch, scratch, match.* Tell them to circle the letters *tch* in each word. ✓

Phonics Objectives

Can students:
- ✓ identify the /r/ and /n/ sounds formed by the letter combinations *wr* and *kn?*
- ✓ read and write words and sentences with silent *k* and *w?*

Language Acquisition Objectives

Can students:
- ✓ use the verbs *write* and *know?*
- ✓ use adjectives *right* and *wrong?*

Students:
- • use homonyms

ESL Standards
- • Goal 1, Standard 3

| wr | Right or Wrong? | kn | Do you know? |

21-9=???
I don't know.

It's wrong.   Mike likes to write.   knee   knife

Circle *right* if the sentence is correct. Circle *wrong* if it is not correct.

1	Students write on a desk.	(right)	wrong
2	Your knee is near your face.	right	wrong
3	Cats can write.	right	wrong
4	Math problems make you think.	right	wrong
5	21−9=11	right	wrong
6	Dogs and cats know math.	right	wrong
7	You can drink milk with a knife.	right	wrong
8	You can make a sandwich with cheese in it.	right	wrong
9	A peach is a fruit.	right	wrong
10	Cats can make a scratch on your hand.	right	wrong
11	A watch goes on your leg.	right	wrong
12	You can catch a ball with a mitt.	right	wrong

74 Unit 8
Digraphs: Silent Letters: /r/wr, /n/kn; Verbs: write, know; Adjectives: right, wrong; Homonyms

---

DEVELOPING PHONEMIC AWARENESS

Ask your class to listen very, very carefully. Move your mouth, but do not make any sound. *What did you hear?* Explain that, in English, sometimes letters stand for no sound at all. Point to your knee and say the word *knee. What letter usually stands for the first sound you hear in the word* knee? (*the letter* n) Explain that the word *knee* starts with the letter *k. Can you hear /k/ in the word* knee? Explain that it is called a "silent *k."* If the *k* were pronounced, the word *knee* would sound like /k/+/nē/. Then point out that the letter *w* is silent when it is combined with *r* as in the word *write.*

USING PAGE 74

Ask students to:
- • point to the letters *wr, kn*
- • locate the words as you say them
- • read aloud and track words with you

Read aloud the title on the page and point out the silent *w* in *wrong* and the silent *k* in *know.* Explain that *right* and *wrong* are opposite adjectives. When would you say, *Is it right or wrong? Do you know?* Tell students that *Do you know?* can be used to ask all sorts of questions. Brainstorm with students questions that can begin with *Do you know,* such as math problems and how-to questions.

Introduce homonyms by pointing out the words *right* and *write* on the page. Explain that even though they sound the same, they are two different words with different meanings. List and explain other homonyms such as *hour/our, to/two, here/hear.*

INCLUDING ALL LEARNERS

Do you know Questions
(Auditory Learners)

Materials: index cards

Write *where, how, when, who,* and *how* on index cards and mix them up. Ask a

student to pick a card and ask a *Do you know* question that includes the question word on the card. (*Do you know when school ends?*) Let each student select a card and ask a *Do you know* question.

Say It!

Teach the class the following chant.

I'm never wrong.
I'm always right.
I'm perfect as can be.
I know it all.
I'm very bright.
Just watch and you can see!

Invite individuals to perform the chant humorously, doing something wrong. ✓

Write It!

Dictate the following words and instruct students to write the word and then either "silent w" or "silent k" as appropriate: *wrong, knee, knife, write, know.* Review the work as a class. ✓

Little Book: *Ask Me a Riddle*

Key Words: beach, nothing, lunch, sandwich, sing, long, song, ding, dong, king, ring, catch, write, what, when

Phonics Objectives

Can students:
✓ listen for the /hw/, /ng/, /ch/, and /r/ sounds?
✓ read words with the letter combinations *wh, ng, ch, tch,* and *wr* in the context of a story?
✓ write words with the letter combinations *wh, ch, tch, ng?*

Language Acquisition Objectives

Can students:
✓ read words in story context?
✓ use riddles?

ESL Standards

• Goal 1, Standard 2

BUILDING BACKGROUND

Say the word *pen* and ask a volunteer what the word means. *The word* pen *can have two different meanings.* Ask if anyone can tell you both meanings. Explain that a *pen* is something you write with and also a fenced-in area. Then ask the riddle, *When can a sheep write his name?* Invite students to come up with answers. Then explain that the answer *When he has a pen* works because a sheep often lives in a fenced-in area, a *pen,* which is the same word for a writing tool.

Tell the class that in the Little Book they are about to make, they will be asked to solve riddles. Encourage them to remember that words can have more than one meaning as they try to solve the riddles.

USING THE LITTLE BOOK

Explain to students that they are going to make a Little Book about riddles. Ask them to remove pages 75 and 76 from their books. Show them how to cut the page on the dotted line with the scissors icon, then fold the pages to make their own eight-page Little Book.

Preview *Ask Me a Riddle* by reading the title aloud to the class. Allow students time to look through the book and examine the pictures. Ask students to follow along and track the words in the Little Book as you read each riddle aloud to them. Ask them to try to guess the answer to each riddle before you read the answers together.

Engage the class in a discussion of each riddle. Ask students to read the riddles aloud to each other and to try to figure out the answer to each riddle. Invite volunteers to explain the solution to each riddle

to the other students. Discuss the multiple meanings of the key word in the riddle. Let students tell riddles of their own that they know and explain their solutions.

Revisit the book. Show how the pictures on the pages help explain the riddle answers. For example, the riddle *When is a fish like a baseball team?* shows a fish catching a fly in a mitt, because the answer is *When he catches flies. Flies* refers to both the insect and balls hit in baseball. Lead the class in a second reading of *Ask Me a Riddle.* This time, ask for volunteers to read aloud one riddle at a time. After each riddle, ask questions to check students' understanding. Here are some examples:

• *What two meanings of the word* wave *are used in the first riddle?*
• *Why does a snake sing a longggg songgggg?*

INCLUDING ALL LEARNERS

Telling Riddles
(Auditory Learners)

Materials: riddle books

Bring in some books of riddles, or take the class on a visit to the library. Ask students to write down a riddle or two that they like. Then invite students to tell their riddles to the rest of the class. More advanced students can write original riddles of their own.

Illustrate a Riddle
(Visual Learners)

Materials: drawing paper, markers or crayons

Ask students to make a new drawing of one of the riddle answers from *Ask Me a Riddle* that also explains the answer. Tell them to also write the riddle on the same piece of paper. Display the illustrations on a bulletin board.

Riddle Time
(Extra Help)

Give students extra time to read *Ask Me a Riddle* quietly. Then divide the students into small groups, and have them take turns telling each other the riddles. Suggest that the students ask or read the riddles to their friends who are native English speakers.

Say It!

Give students time to read the story aloud. Then engage the class in a discussion about words they read in the story. *What letter sounds do you know in the words? Which words have the digraphs* wh, ng, ch, tch, wr? ✔

Write It!

Challenge students to look through their Little Book *Ask Me a Riddle* and list the words with *wh, ng, ch, tch,* and *wr.* Then ask students to do the following:

- Circle all the words that begin with the letters *wh.*
- Draw a box around all the words that end with *ch* or *tch.*
- Underline all the words that end with *ng.*
- Star all words that start with *wr.*

When they are finished, review the activity as a class. ✔

Family Connection

 Send home the Little Book *Ask Me a Riddle.* Encourage students to read the riddles to a family member.

/hw/ wh
Whistle for Willie by Ezra Jack Keats

/hw/ wh, /ng/ ng
The Whale's Song by Dyan Sheldon

/ng/ -ing
King Bidgood's in the Bathtub by Audrey Wood

/ch/ ch
Peter's Chair by Ezra Jack Keats

/ch/ tch
Horton Hatches An Egg by Dr. Seuss

/n/ kn
The Know-Nothings by Michele Sobel Spirn

/r/ wr
Don't Forget to Write by Martina Selway

Review

Digraphs: wh, ng, ch, tch, wr, kn

Phonics Objectives

Can students:
✓ listen for the /hw/, /ng/, /ch/, /r/, and /n/ sounds?
✓ identify the /hw/, /ng/, /ch/, /r/, and /n/ sounds formed by different letter combinations?
✓ read and write words with the letter combinations *wh, ng, ch, tch, wr,* and *kn*?

Language Acquisition Objectives

Can students:
✓ use present progressive verbs?
✓ use rhyming words?

ESL Standards

• Goal 2, Standard 3

Review: Words that Rhyme

~~dish~~	whale	scratch	wheat
wrong	shine	king	knee	know
that	shake	sheep	shoe
write	when	bath	

Write the rhyming word from the box on the line next to each word below.

1. fish ___dish___
2. then _____
3. cat _____
4. snake _____
5. ring _____
6. long _____
7. line _____
8. math _____
9. meat _____
10. white _____
11. blue _____
12. sleep _____
13. three _____
14. snow _____
15. snail _____
16. catch _____

Review of Digraphs; Rhymes **Unit 8 77**

BUILDING BACKGROUND

Write the following words on the chalkboard: *whale, king, lunch, match.* Ask the class to say the word that ends with *ng,* begins with *wh,* ends with *ch,* and ends with *tch.* Then write the words *know* and *wrong* on the chalkboard. Ask a volunteer to read them aloud and circle the silent letter.

Review with the class how words with the same ending sound are called rhyming words. Ask students to think of words they know that rhyme with the words from the unit that are on the board. Write their correct suggestions beneath the words with which they rhyme. Invite students to come up with examples of other rhyming words.

USING THE REVIEW PAGE

Ask students to:
• point to the letters *wh, ng, tch, wr, kn*
• locate the words as you say them
• read aloud with you and track words

Read aloud the title of the page, *Words that Rhyme,* and ask students to repeat it. Review the exercise as a class or divide the class into pairs or small groups and let them compare their pages.

INCLUDING ALL LEARNERS

Rhyming Concentration
(Kinesthetic/Visual Learners)

Materials: index cards

Write the following words on the chalkboard and on index cards: *when, then, king, ring, know, throw, wheat, eat, catch, match, knee, three.* Mix up the cards and place them facedown. The players alternate turning over two cards and reading the words aloud. If the words rhyme, the player keeps the cards. The player with the most cards at the end of the game wins. An alternate game is for players to turn over only one card, and if he or she can come up with a rhyming word, he or she keeps the card.

Say It!

Teach students the following chant:

> I like to do many things, you know.
> Munching on peaches, walking in snow.
> Watching baseball, singing a song.
> These are all things that can't go wrong!

Recite the chant as a class. Then ask students to make up their own chants or rhymes with *-ing* verbs describing things they like to do. ☑

Write It!

Ask students to write sentences of their own containing some of the words in the box on the page. ☑

UNIT 9

r-Controlled Vowels: ar, er, ir, ur

r-Controlled Vowels: /är/ ar

Key Words: farm, barn, garden, car, park, star, dark, arm

Phonics Objectives

Can students:
- ✓ listen for the /är/ sound?
- ✓ identify the /är/ sound formed by the letter combination *ar*?
- ✓ read and write words and sentences with the /är/ sound?

Language Acquisition Objectives

Can students:
- ✓ use the verb *to be: are*?
- ✓ use farm words: *barn, farm*?

ESL Standards

- Goal 2, Standard 1
- Goal 3, Standard 3

UNIT 9 r-Controlled Vowels: ar, er, ir, ur | ar **The Farm**

farm: barn and garden | Stars are bright in the dark.

a car in a park | arm

Match the sentences with the pictures.

1. A barn is on the farm.
2. Kate's arm is inside the car.
3. The park has a garden and a swing.
4. The sky is dark when it rains.
5. The car has a star on the front.

78 Unit 9
r-Controlled Vowels: /är/ar; Verb: are

DEVELOPING PHONEMIC AWARENESS

Hold up your arm and say the word *arm,* stressing the /är/ sound. Invite the class to raise their arms and say *arm* after you. Explain that in English the letters *a* and *r* together often represent the /är/ sound. Then point out that when the letter *r* follows a vowel, the vowel sound sometimes changes.

Ask students to listen as you say some words. Have them repeat each word and, if it has the /är/ sound as in *arm,* they should wave their arms. Say the following words: <u>far</u>m, <u>far</u>, time, goat, <u>gar</u>den, dog, <u>dark</u>, boat, <u>barn</u>, stand, <u>star</u>.

USING PAGE 78

Ask students to:
- point to the letters *ar*
- locate the words as you say them
- read aloud and track words with you

Point out the sentence *Stars are bright in the dark* in the box on the page. Explain that the verb *are* is used when talking or writing about more than one thing. Hold up a pencil and say, *The pencil <u>is</u> yellow.* Then hold up a few pencils and say, *The pencils <u>are</u> yellow.* Invite students to discuss how the verb *to be* is expressed in other languages. Conjugate the verb for more advanced students.

INCLUDING ALL LEARNERS

"Ar" Stars
(Kinesthetic/Visual Learners)

Materials: white and black construction paper, scissors, crayons or markers, pins

Ask students to cut stars out of white paper. Write *ar* words on the board: *farm, barn, garden, car, park, star, dark, arm.* Then ask students to draw a picture of one of the *ar* words from the board or one of their own on their stars. Place black paper on a bulletin board for students to pin stars on the "night sky."

Say It!

Teach the song "Twinkle, Twinkle, Little Star." 🎵

Twinkle, twinkle, little star.
How I wonder what you are.
Up above the world so high
Like a diamond in the sky.
Twinkle, twinkle, little star.
How I wonder what you are.

Ask students to raise their arms every time they say a word with the /är/ sound. ✓

Write It!

Write *star, car, barn,* and *park* on the chalkboard. Read the class the following riddles. After each riddle, ask students to write the *ar* word answer.

1. I am a place with swings, slides, and picnic tables. *(park)*
2. On a farm, horses live in me. *(barn)*
3. I am bright in the night sky. *(star)*
4. You can go for a drive in me. *(car)* ✓

r-Controlled Vowels: /ėr/ er

Key Words: summer, winter, weather, mother, sister, her, father, brother

Phonics Objectives
Can students:
- ✓ listen for and identify the /ėr/ sound formed by *er*?
- ✓ read and write words and sentences with the /ėr/ sound?

Language Acquisition Objectives
Can students:
- ✓ use family words?

Students:
- use the pronoun *her*
- use words for weather and seasons.

ESL Standards
- Goal 2, Standard 2

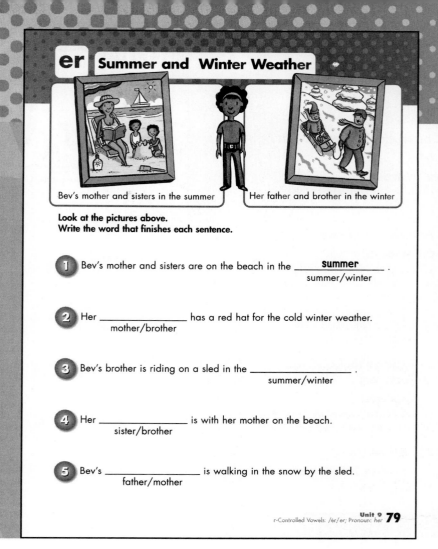

er Summer and Winter Weather

Bev's mother and sisters in the summer   Her father and brother in the winter

Look at the pictures above.
Write the word that finishes each sentence.

1. Bev's mother and sisters are on the beach in the ____**summer**____ .
   summer/winter

2. Her _____ has a red hat for the cold winter weather.
   mother/brother

3. Bev's brother is riding on a sled in the _____ .
   summer/winter

4. Her _____ is with her mother on the beach.
   sister/brother

5. Bev's _____ is walking in the snow by the sled.
   father/mother

r-Controlled Vowels: /ėr/er; Pronoun: *her* **Unit 9 79**

BUILDING BACKGROUND

Write the word *summer* and *winter* on the chalkboard. Read them aloud for the class and ask students to repeat them after you. Point out that the letter combination *er* makes the /ėr/ sound. Explain that these are two seasons of the year. Ask which is the hottest season and which is the coldest season in the United States.

Ask students to write the word *summer* on one side of a piece of paper and *winter* on the other side. Tell them to listen carefully as you name some activities. If the activity takes place in warm weather, have them hold up the word *summer* and say, *Summer!* If it takes place in cold weather, tell them to hold up *winter* and say, *Winter!* Use the following activities: *swimming, skiing, ice skating, baseball, sunbathing, snow boarding, waterskiing, ice fishing.* Engage students in a discussion of other things they do in the winter and summer.

USING PAGE 79

Ask students to:
- point to the letters *er*
- locate the words as you say them
- read aloud and track words with you

Point out and say the words *mother, sister, father,* and *brother* on the page and stress the /ėr/ sound. Explain that they are all words for family members. Point out that the pronoun *her* means *Bev's.* Bring in photos of your family to share with the class. Invite students to make and label diagrams or family trees of their families.

INCLUDING ALL LEARNERS

Summer and Winter Collages
(Kinesthetic/Visual Learners)

Materials: magazines, clothing catalogs, scissors, construction paper, glue

Ask students to look through the magazines and cut out pictures of summer and winter things. Instruct them to label one side of the construction paper "Winter" and the other side "Summer," then glue the pictures on the appropriate side.

Say It!
 Teach the following rhyme.

> Bobby has three sisters.
> He is the only brother.
> His father and his mother say
> They will soon have another!

Ask students to clap their hands each time they say a word with the /ėr/ sound. ✔

Write It!
Write the words *brother, sister, father,* and *mother* on the chalkboard. Then read the following sentences to the class. Ask students to write the name of the family member for each sentence.

1. She is married to my father. *(mother)*
2. Her brother has the same mother as she does. *(sister)*
3. He is married to my mother. *(father)*
4. His sister has the same father as he does. *(brother)* ✔

r-Controlled Vowels: /èr/ ir, ur

Key Words: bird, turtle, girl, sunburn, hurt, purple, shirt, nurse

Phonics Objectives

Can students:
- ✓ listen for the /èr/ sound?
- ✓ identify the /èr/ sound formed by the letter combinations *ir* and *ur?*
- ✓ read and write words and sentences with the /èr/ sound?

Language Acquisition Objectives:

Can students:
- ✓ use animal words: *bird, turtle?*
- ✓ use safety words: *nurse, sunburn?*

ESL Standards

- Goal 2, Standard 1
- Goal 3, Standard 2

---

ir ur Birds and Turtles

bird   turtle   The girl's sunburn hurts.   a purple T-shirt   nurse

Circle *yes* if the sentence is true. Circle *no* if the sentence is not true.

1	A turtle can fly.	yes	(no)
2	Birds can fly.	yes	no
3	Nan's sunburn hurts.	yes	no
4	The turtle is purple.	yes	no
5	Nan is a girl.	yes	no
6	Nan has a red shirt.	yes	no
7	The nurse has a purple dress.	yes	no
8	The T-shirt is purple.	yes	no

DEVELOPING PHONEMIC AWARENESS

Display a picture of a bird and say the word *bird,* stressing the /èr/ sound. *What can birds do that we can't do?* Invite students to pretend to fly, flapping their arms as wings, and say *bird* three times. Ask students to listen as you say some words. Tell them to repeat each word after you and, if it has the same /èr/ sound as in *bird,* flap their "wings" like a bird. Use the following words: <u>girl</u>, goal, tall, <u>turtle</u>, <u>shirt</u>, noise, <u>nurse</u>, barn, <u>burn</u>, hand, <u>hurt</u>.

USING PAGE 80

Ask students to:
- point to the letters *ir* and *ur*
- locate the words as you say them
- read aloud and track words with you

Point out the word *sunburn* on the page and read it aloud. Explain that *sunburn* is a compound word made of two smaller words. Ask a volunteer to say what those words are. Point out that you can tell the meaning of a compound word by exploring the meanings of the smaller words. Ask students to discuss meanings of the smaller words in these words: *milkshake, classroom, basketball, bedroom.*

INCLUDING ALL LEARNERS

Turtle and Bird Race
(Auditory/Kinesthetic Learners)

Materials: index cards, bird picture, turtle picture, large paper bag

Write the words *bird, turtle, girl, sunburn, shirt, nurse, hurt,* and *dirt* on index cards and mix them in the bag. Put the bird and the turtle pictures on the chalk rail and write the numbers one through ten on the board to mark off steps of a race. Ask a volunteer to pick a card from the bag and read the word aloud. If it has the /èr/ sound spelled *ir,* move the bird forward one space. If the /èr/ sound is spelled *ur,* move the turtle forward one space. Invite

students to come up one at a time, pick a card, and read it aloud. The first animal to reach the tenth space is the winner!

Say It!

 Teach your class the following chant.

My turtle cannot fetch a stick.
He cannot say a word.
He cannot run, or jump, or play
Or fly high like a bird.

No, there aren't many things
My turtle can do well.
I guess that's why he spends his day
Curled up inside his shell.

Ask students which words contain the /èr/ sound. ☑

Write It!

Dictate a list of words that have the /èr/ sound. After you say each word, ask students to write it down. Use the following words: *hurt, bird, turtle, girl, sunburn, shirt, purple.* ☑

Little Book: *The Farm*

Key Words: far, summer, garden, her, sister, father, barn, girl, are, sunburn, brother, park, mother, arm, dark, thunder, shirt, weather, bird

Phonics Objectives

Can students:

✓ listen for the /är/ and /ėr/ sounds?
✓ read words with the letter combinations *ar, er, ir,* and *ur* in the context of a story?
✓ write words with the letter combinations *ar, er, ir, ur?*

Language Acquisition Objectives

Can students:

✓ read words in story context?

ESL Standards

• Goal 1, Standard 2
• Goal 3, Standard 1

DEVELOPING PHONEMIC AWARENESS

As a warm-up for the next Little Book, teach your class the following chant.

> There's a barn on the farm.
> On the farm, farm, farm.
> There's a cow in the barn.
> In the barn, barn, barn.

Invite volunteers to model blending the sounds in words from the chant. For example, ask a student to say the word *farm* and demonstrate blending the sounds /f/, /är/, and /m/ together.

Brainstorm with students different things you could find in a barn. Then help them make up new verses to the chant. Explain that the story in the next Little Book takes place on a farm.

USING THE LITTLE BOOK

Explain to students that they are going to make a Little Book about a farm. Ask them to remove pages 81 and 82 from their books. Show them how to cut the page on the dotted line with the scissors icon, then fold the pages to make their own eight-page Little Book.

Preview *The Farm* by reading the title aloud to the class. Allow students time to look through the book and examine the pictures. Ask students to follow along and track the words in the Little Book as you read the story aloud to them.

Engage the class in the story. Draw upon students' experiences and feelings about the story to spark their interest. Ask them questions such as *Did you ever live on a farm? What are farms like in other coun-*

tries? Have you ever been in the sun too long? What happened? Have you ever been caught outside in a rainstorm? What happened? Have you ever seen a symbol with a wheelchair? Where?

Revisit the story. Lead the class in a second reading of *The Farm*. This time, ask for volunteers to read aloud one page at a time. After each page is read, ask questions focusing on the content of the story. Here are some examples:

• *What are Nan and her sister doing on the farm?*
• *Who is in the wheelchair?*
• *What happens to Nan's arms?*
• *Why do the girls go into the barn?*

INCLUDING ALL LEARNERS

Act Out the Story: *The Farm*
(Kinesthetic/Auditory Learners)

Ask for two volunteers to act out the story *The Farm.* Assign the roles of Nan and her sister. The student who plays Nan's sister can sit in a chair and pretend to wheel herself around. Discuss with the class why Nan's sister is in a wheelchair and explain the word *disabled. Do you know any disabled people?*

Invite the volunteers to act out the story as you read it aloud to the class. Students can make thunder and rain sound effects for the storm. Encourage the students to mime working in a garden as the story begins. (Since Nan has some lines of dialogue in the story, you may want to rehearse the spoken lines.)

When you are done, call on a new pair of actors. Ask a volunteer to read the story aloud while the actors perform it. Encourage other groups of students to perform the story for the class.

Illustrate the Story
(Visual Learners)

Materials: drawing paper, markers or crayons

Ask the class to make their own drawings of one of the text pages from *The Farm.* When they are finished, display the illustrations on a bulletin board under copies of their corresponding text pages. Extend the activity by asking students to draw pictures of their own experiences getting sunburned or being stuck outside in the rain.

Story Time
(Extra Help)

Give students extra time to read the story quietly. Ask students to give summaries of what happened in the story. Then encourage them to think about a time when their plans were changed because of bad weather. Invite students to share their stories with the rest of the class.

It is summer on the farm.

Nan is in the garden with her sister.

Her father is in the barn.

The sun is hot, and the girls are getting a sunburn.

"I don't like this hot weather," says Nan.

Nan's brother is not at the farm today.

He is playing baseball at the park.

Nan's mother is with him.

"Let's go inside," says Nan. "My arms are getting red."

Say It!

Give students time to read the story aloud. Then engage the class in a discussion about words they read in the story. *What letter sounds do you know in the words? Which words have the r-controlled vowels ar, er, ir, ur?* ✔

Write It!

Ask students to fold a paper into four columns and label the columns: *ar, er, ir, ur.* Then tell them to look through their Little Book *The Farm* and list the *r*-controlled words in the appropriate columns: ✔

Family Connection

Send home the Little Book *The Farm.* Encourage students to read the book to a family member.

BOOK CORNER

/är/ ar
Old MacDonald Had a Farm by Abner Graboff

/är/ ar, /èr/ er
Farmer Duck by Martin Waddell

/èr/ er
Seven Chinese Brothers by Margaret Mahy

/èr/ ir
Harry the Dirty Dog by Margaret Bloy Graham

/èr/ ur
The Great Big Enormous Turnip by Alexei Tolstoy and Helen Oxenbury

/èr/ ur
Turtle Tale by Frank Asch

Review

r-Controlled Vowels: ar, er, ir, ur

Key Words: over, under, before, after, water

Phonics Objectives

Can students:

✓ listen for the /är/ and /èr/ sounds?

✓ identify the /är/ and /èr/ sounds formed by different letter combinations?

✓ read and write words with ar, er, ir, and ur?

Language Acquisition Objectives

Can students:

✓ use the prepositions: over/under, before/after?

ESL Standards

• Goal 2, Standard 2

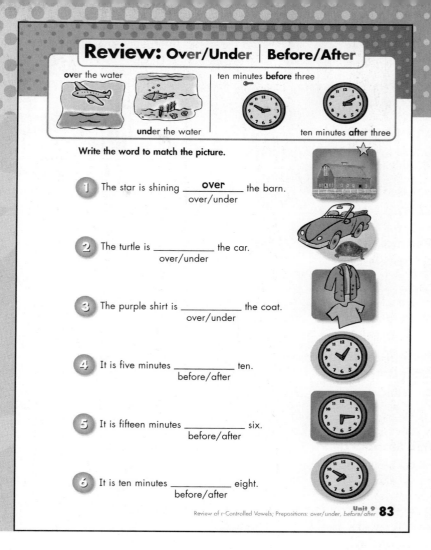

Review: Over/Under | Before/After

over the water · under the water · ten minutes **before** three · ten minutes **after** three

Write the word to match the picture.

1. The star is shining ___**over**___ the barn.
   over/under

2. The turtle is _____ the car.
   over/under

3. The purple shirt is _____ the coat.
   over/under

4. It is five minutes _____ ten.
   before/after

5. It is fifteen minutes _____ six.
   before/after

6. It is ten minutes _____ eight.
   before/after

Review of r-Controlled Vowels; Prepositions: over/under, before/after **83**

Building Background

Bring in a bowl and a small ball. Place the bowl facedown and put the ball under the bowl. Say, *The ball is under the bowl.* Then say, *The bowl is over the ball.* Move the ball over the bowl and say, *Now the ball is over the bowl. The bowl is under the ball.* Ask a student to put the ball over or under the bowl and invite a volunteer to say where the ball is using the prepositions *over* and *under.*

Using the Review Page

Ask students to:

• point to the letters *er*
• locate the words as you say them
• read aloud and track words with you

Ask the class to look at the title of the page. Read *over/under* aloud and invite students to repeat it. Use the pictures of the plane over the water and the fish

under the water in the box to review the prepositions *over* and *under.* Then read *before/after* aloud and ask students to repeat it. Explain the prepositions *before* and *after* using the pictures of the clock in the box. Use a teaching clock to tell time by showing and saying minutes *before* and *after* the hour.

Including All Learners

Red Rover, Red Rover
(Kinesthetic Learners)

Ask students to get in two parallel lines some distance apart. Students in line 1 decide whom to call over from line 2. They join hands and chant "Red rover, red rover, let _____ come over!" If the named person can run and break through line 1, he or she joins line 1. If not, he or she returns to line 2. Alternate the lines.

Say It!

Teach the song *One More River.* Preview words that students might not know.

Old Noah built himself an ark,
One more river to cross,
He built it out of hickory bark,
One more river to cross.

Ask students to sing the song and clap each time they hear /èr/ and /är/ sounds. ✓

Write It!

Write the following sentences on the chalkboard. Ask students to use *over, under, before,* or *after* to complete the sentences.

1. When it rains, stay _____ an umbrella. *(under)*
2. The bird flew _____ the school. *(over)*
3. Four comes _____ five. *(before)*
4. Six comes _____ five. *(after)* ✓

UNIT 10

Diphthongs: oo, ou, ow, oy, oi

Diphthongs: /ü/ oo

Key Words: oops, shoot, hoop, food, balloon, boot, school

Phonics Objectives

Can students:
✓ listen for the /ü/ sound?
✓ identify the /ü/ sound formed by the letter combination *oo*?
✓ read and write words and sentences with the /ü/ sound?

Language Acquisition Objectives

Students:
• use the verb *shoot*
• use exclamation points

ESL Standards

• Goal 2, Standard 2
• Goal 3, Standard 1

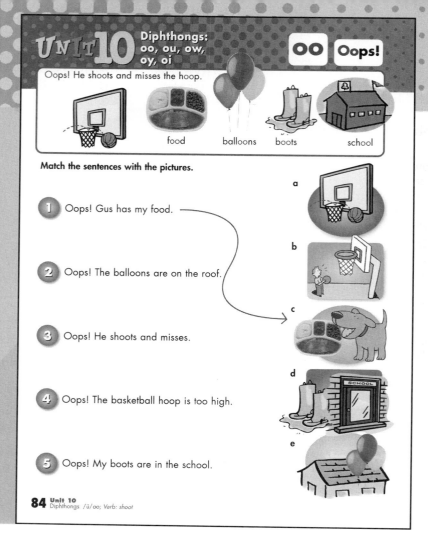

DEVELOPING PHONEMIC AWARENESS

Get students' attention, then drop something on the floor and say, *Oops!* Tell students that *oops* is an expression used when you make a mistake. Explain that the /ü/ sound in *oops* appears in many words in English, for example the word *shoot.* Say the word *shoot* and pretend to shoot a basketball into a hoop.

Ask students to listen as you say some words. Tell them to repeat each word and, if it has the /ü/ sound as in *shoot,* pretend to shoot a basketball into a hoop. Use the following words: *top, hop, hoop, beat, boot, should, shoot, food, feed, school.*

USING PAGE 84

Ask students to:
• point to the letters *oo*
• locate the words as you say them
• read aloud and track words with you

Ask students to look at the title of the page, *Oops!* Read it loudly and point out the exclamation point. Explain that an exclamation point at the end of a sentence means the sentence should be read with excitement. Write some of the sentences from the page on the board and ask volunteers to read them aloud. Then change the periods to exclamation points and ask students to read the sentences aloud with more excitement.

INCLUDING ALL LEARNERS

Pop an "Oo" Balloon!
(Kinesthetic Learners)

Materials: balloons, small slips of paper, pin

Write the following words on small slips of paper: *shoot, hoop, food, balloon, boot, school.* Put the slips of paper inside uninflated balloons. Then blow the balloons up and tie them off. Ask volunteers to pop a balloon with the pin and then use the *oo* word on the slip of paper in a sentence.

Say It!

 Teach the following rhyme. 🎧

One boot, two boots
Boop-boop-a-doop
Old boot, new boot
Boop-boop-a-doop
My boot, your boot
Boop-boop-a-doop
Down on the floor boot
Boop-boop-a-doop!

After the class has learned the rhyme, ask students to brainstorm additional lines with the /ü/ sound. ✓

Write It!

Write the following words on the chalkboard: *hoop, food, balloon, boots, school.* Ask students to write three sentences, each containing one of the *oo* words. For extra credit, students can write a fourth sentence that uses two of the *oo* words. ✓

Diphthongs: /ou/ *ou*

Key Words: loud, sound, shout, mouth, bounce, outside, around, house

Phonics Objectives

Can students:
- ✓ listen for the /ou/ sound?
- ✓ identify the /ou/ sound formed by the letter combination *ou*?
- ✓ read and write words and sentences with the /ou/ sound?

Language Acquisition Objectives

Can students:
- ✓ use the verb *bounce*?

Students:
- use the preposition *around*
- use words for body parts: *mouth*

ESL Standards
- Goal 2, Standard 1

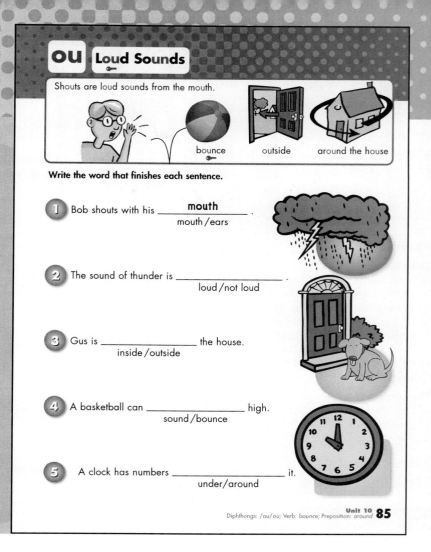

ou | **Loud Sounds**

Shouts are loud sounds from the mouth.

bounce   outside   around the house

Write the word that finishes each sentence.

1. Bob shouts with his ___**mouth**___ .
   mouth / ears

2. The sound of thunder is _____ .
   loud / not loud

3. Gus is _____ the house.
   inside / outside

4. A basketball can _____ high.
   sound / bounce

5. A clock has numbers _____ it.
   under / around

Diphthongs: /ou/ou; Verb: bounce; Preposition: around **Unit 10 85**

DEVELOPING PHONEMIC AWARENESS

Say, *I am talking loudly,* in a loud voice. Ask students to say the word *loud* very loudly. Say the word *loud* and model blending the sounds of the letters together: /l/, /ou/, /d/. Explain that the letters *ou* together often stand for the /ou/ sound they hear in *loud.*

Ask students to listen very carefully as you say some words. Tell them to repeat each word. If the word has the same /ou/ sound as in *loud,* they should say the word loudly. Use the following words: *boat, bounce, ship, shout, his, hop, hope, house, mouth, sound, inside, outside.*

USING PAGE 85

Ask students to:
- point to the letters *ou*
- locate the words as you say them
- read aloud and track words with you

Ask students to look at the word *bounce* and its illustration in the box. Read the word aloud and demonstrate the verb *bounce.* Invite students to name things that *bounce. (ball, children on trampoline)* Then point out the preposition *around* in *around the house.* Explain that *around* means "on all sides." Ask volunteers to name things that are *around* them.

INCLUDING ALL LEARNERS

Explore Sounds
(Auditory Learners)

Ask the class to sit very quietly and listen very carefully to all the sounds in the classroom. As they listen, encourage them to listen to soft sounds that are far, far away. Afterward, engage the class in a discussion of the different sounds they were able to hear and list them on the board. To continue the activity, take the class to different locations in the school or outside the school and let students identify the various sounds.

Say It!

 Teach your class the following chant.

My mouth makes sounds.
My mouth says words.
My mouth can whistle
Like the birds.
My mouth's between
my nose and chin.
And when I'm happy
My mouth can grin!

After you recite the chant as a class, invite individuals to perform it. ✓

Write It!

Write *sounds, shout, bounce,* and *house* on the chalkboard. Read the following riddles and ask students to write the *ou* word answers.

1. People live in me. *(house)*
2. Some of these are loud and some are very quiet. *(sounds)*
3. You do this with a ball. *(bounce)*
4. You do this when you need help. *(shout)* ✓

Diphthongs: /ou/ *ow*

Key Words: how, now, brown, cow, town, down, clown, crown

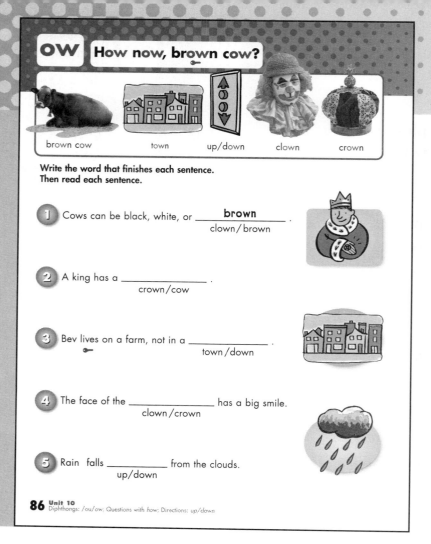

OW How now, brown cow?

brown cow · town · up/down · clown · crown

Write the word that finishes each sentence. Then read each sentence.

1. Cows can be black, white, or ___**brown**___ .
   clown / brown

2. A king has a _____ .
   crown / cow

3. Bev lives on a farm, not in a _____ .
   town / down

4. The face of the _____ has a big smile.
   clown / crown

5. Rain falls _____ from the clouds.
   up/down

86 Unit 10
Diphthongs: /ou/ow; Questions with how; Directions: up/down

Phonics Objectives

Can students:
✓ listen for the /ou/ sound?
✓ identify the /ou/ sound formed by the letter combination *ow*?
✓ read and write words and sentences with the /ou/ sound?

Language Acquisition Objectives

Can students:
✓ use the question word *how*?
✓ use rhymes?
✓ use color words: *brown*?

ESL Standards

• Goal 2, Standard 1

DEVELOPING PHONEMIC AWARENESS

Sit in a chair in front of the class. Say the word *up* and stand up. Then say the word *down*, stressing the /ou/ sound, and sit down. Ask students to say *up* and stand up, then *down* and sit down with you. Point out that the letters *ow* sometimes stand for the /ou/ sound as in *down*.

Ask students to stand as you say some words and to repeat each word. If the word has the same /ou/ sound as in *down*, they should sit down, then stand back up. Use the following words: _cow_, _now_, new, clear, _clown_, bone, _brown_, _crown_, hot, _how_.

USING PAGE 86

Ask students to:
• point to the letters *ow*
• locate the words as you say them
• read aloud and track words with you

Read the title of the page, *How now, brown cow?* Explain that *how* is a question word that is often used to ask the way something is done. Write *How do you put on a shoe?* on the board and read it aloud. Invite students to think of other questions beginning with *how*. Write *How are you?* on the board. Invite the students to practice saying *How are you?* to each other. *How do people say* How are you? *in other countries?*

INCLUDING ALL LEARNERS

"Ow" Tongue Twisters
(Auditory Learners)

How now, brown cow? Ask students to say it quickly. Explain that it is a "tongue twister," a sentence that is tricky to say. Introduce other tongue twisters using *ow* words, such as *The queen's round crown fell down.* Ask students to make up their own tongue twisters with *ow* words for you and other students to try.

Say It!

Teach this chant.
How do birds fly?
How do bees sting?
How do cows make milk?
How do dogs bark?
How do cats purr?
How do worms make silk?

Ask students to come up with additional *how* questions. ✓

Write It!

Write the following incomplete sentences on the chalkboard. Ask students to write down each sentence and fill in the blank with a word that makes sense and rhymes with the underlined word.

1. I don't know <u>how</u> you milk a _____. *(cow)*
2. When he falls <u>down</u>, we laugh at the _____. *(clown)*
3. When the king comes to <u>town</u> he wears a _____. *(crown)*
4. The streets are <u>brown</u> in my home _____. *(town)* ✓

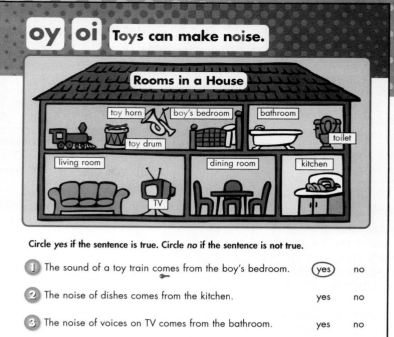

oy **oi** **Toys can make noise.**

Rooms in a House

toy horn   boy's bedroom   bathroom

toy drum   toilet

living room   dining room   kitchen

TV

Circle *yes* if the sentence is true. Circle *no* if the sentence is not true.

1. The sound of a toy train comes from the boy's bedroom.   (yes)   no
2. The noise of dishes comes from the kitchen.   yes   no
3. The noise of voices on TV comes from the bathroom.   yes   no
4. The sound of water comes from the living room.   yes   no
5. The beat of a toy drum comes from the dining room.   yes   no
6. The toot of a toy horn comes from the boy's bedroom.   yes   no
7. The boy's bed is in the kitchen.   yes   no
8. The toilet is in the bathroom.   yes   no

Unit 10 **87**
Diphthongs: /oi/ oy, oi

Diphthongs: /oi/ oy, oi

Key Words: toy, noise, boy, toilet

Phonics Objectives

Can students:
✓ listen for the /oi/ sound?
✓ identify the /oi/ sound formed by the letter combinations *oy* and *oi?*
✓ read and write words and sentences with the /oi/ sound?

Language Acquisition Objectives

Can students:
✓ identify the names of rooms in a house?

ESL Standards

• Goal 2, Standard 2
• Goal 3, Standard 1

Developing Phonemic Awareness

Bring in an object that makes noise, such as a tambourine, rattle, or drum. Make a noise with the object, then say the word *noise*. Explain that there are all kinds of noises—in fact, anything we can hear is a noise. Say, *Toys can make noise*, stressing the /oi/ sound in *toys* and *noise*. Use the words *toys* and *noise* to model oral blending.

Ask students to listen as you say some words and to repeat each word. Then, if the word has the /oi/ sound as in *noise*, they should make a noise with their hands, feet, or an object like a pencil. You can use the following words: *bug, boy, toy, tie, tub, toilet, van, voice.*

Using Page 87

Ask students to:
• point to the letters *oy* and *oi*
• locate the words as you say them
• read aloud and track words with you

Read aloud the names of the rooms in the house on the page. Point out the things in each of the rooms. Then engage the students in a discussion about the function of each room. Ask students to talk about and draw the rooms in the apartment or house where they live now or in other countries where they used to live. Invite students to compare what houses are like in different countries.

Including All Learners

Toy Collages
(Visual/Kinesthetic Learners)

Materials: newspapers, catalogs, scissors, construction paper, glue

Divide the class into pairs or small groups. Distribute the materials and ask the groups to look through the magazines or catalogues and cut out pictures of different types of toys. Instruct them to discuss favorites and glue the pictures onto construction paper. Invite the groups to share their collages with the class.

Say It!

 Teach this chant. 🎧

Make a noise!
Clap. Clap. Clap.
Louder noise!
Stomp. Stomp. Stomp.
Softer noise.
Tap. Tap. Tap.
Just the girls!
Clap. Clap. Clap.
Just the boys!
Clap. Clap. Clap.

Have your class clap, stomp, and tap as they recite the chant. ✓

Write It!

 Dictate the following words to students: *toy, boy, noise, voice*. Then, ask students to complete the following sentences using the words.

1. He speaks in a loud _____. *(voice)*
2. She toots on a ____ horn. *(toy)*
3. Thunder makes a loud _____. *(noise)*
4. He is a five-year-old _____. *(boy)* ✓

Review

Diphthongs: *oo, ou, ow, oy, oi*

Key Word: owl

Phonics Objectives

Can students:
- ✓ listen for the /ü/, /ou/, and /oi/ sounds?
- ✓ identify the /ü/, /ou/, and /oi/ sounds formed by different letter combinations?
- ✓ read and write words with the /ü/, /ou/, and /oi/ sounds?

Language Acquisition Objectives

Can students:
- ✓ use onomatopoeia?
- ✓ identify animal sounds?

ESL Standards
- Goal 2, Standard 3

Review: How do animals sound?

HOOO, HOOO!   BOW, WOW   MEOW   CROAK, CROAK

owl   ~~cow~~   dog   duck   cat   pig   frog   sheep

Write the animal name from the box above that answers each riddle.

1. I say MOOOO. I am big and brown. I give milk.   I am a __**COW**__ .

2. I say BOW WOW. I can live in a house or outside.   I am a _____ .

3. I say QUACK, QUACK. I swim in ponds. I can fly.   I am a _____ .

4. I say MEOW, MEOW. I eat birds. I eat mice.   I am a _____ .

5. I say OINK, OINK. I live on a farm. I eat corn.   I am a _____ .

6. I say HOOO, HOOO. I fly at night. I have big eyes.   I am an _____ .

7. I say BAAA, BAAA. I live on a farm. I eat grass.   I am a _____ .

8. I say CROAK, CROAK. I am green. I can swim.   I am a _____ .

88 Unit 10
Review of Diphthongs

BUILDING BACKGROUND

Ask the class if any of them have pets. Invite students to talk about their pets. Then ask, *What kind of sounds do your pets make?* Encourage students to try to imitate the sounds that their pets make.

Introduce the concept of onomatopoeia. Explain that some English words get their name from the sounds they represent. As an example, say the word *quack*. Explain that this is the word for the sound a duck makes. Ask students what sounds animals make in other languages.

USING THE REVIEW PAGE

Ask students to:
- point to the letters *ow, ou*
- locate the words as you say them
- read aloud and track words with you

Read the title of the page, *How do animals sound?*, aloud and ask students to repeat it. Review the words for animals in the box. *What sounds do you think each of these animals makes?* Then read aloud and track the sounds in each sentence before students try to answer the riddles.

INCLUDING ALL LEARNERS

Sound Like Animals
(Auditory Learners)

Materials: index cards

On index cards, write the names of the animals from the box on the page. Then shuffle the cards and ask a volunteer to select one of the cards at random. Challenge the student to make the sound of the animal while the rest of the class tries to guess what the animal is. The first student to guess correctly gets to pick the next card.

Say It!

Teach students the song "She'll Be Comin' Round the Mountain."

She'll be comin' round the
  mountain when she comes.
Toot! Toot!

She'll be comin' round the
  mountain when she comes.
Toot! Toot!
She'll be comin' round the
  mountain,
She'll be comin' round the
  mountain,
She'll be comin' round the
  mountain when she comes.
Toot! Toot!

Sing the song as a class and ask students to clap when they hear the /ou/ or /ü/ sounds. ✓

Write It!

Write the following words on the board: *cow, oink, outside, toy.* Ask students to listen as you read aloud the following sentences and write the answer to complete each.

1. The cat plays with a _____. *(toy)*
2. A pig makes the sound _____. *(oink)*
3. Owls live _____. *(outside)*
4. I say *moo* 'cause I'm a _____. *(cow)* ✓

Little Book: *The Big Game*

Key Words: school, boy, shout, hoop, toot, down, floor, shoot, oops, throw, around, outside, bounce, food, balloon, crown, clown

Phonics Objectives

Can students:

✓ listen for the /ü/, /ou/, and /oi/ sounds?
✓ read words with the letter combinations *oo, ou, ow, oi,* and *oy* in the context of a story?
✓ write words with the letter combinations *oo, ou, ow, oy?*

Language Acquisition Objectives

Can students:

✓ read words in story context?

ESL Standards

• Goal 1, Standard 2

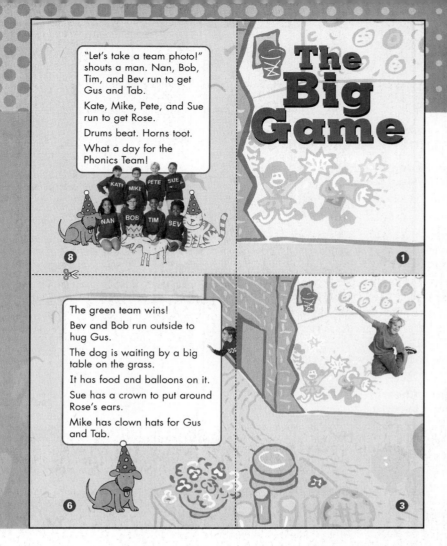

DEVELOPING PHONEMIC AWARENESS

As a warm-up for the next Little Book, teach your class the following cheer. Explain the words *steal* and *block* for the students. Invite volunteers to model blending the sounds in these words.

> Go team!
> Win, win, win!
> Shoot that ball!
> Get it in!
> Steal the ball!
> Block that throw.
> Win the game.
> Go team go!

Invite groups of students to present the cheer as if they were boy and girl cheerleaders at a big game. Tell the class that in the next Little Book, they will read about an exciting basketball game.

USING THE LITTLE BOOK

Explain to students that they are going to make a Little Book about a basketball game. Ask them to remove pages 89 and 90 from their books. Show them how to cut the page on the dotted line with the scissors icon, then fold the pages to make their own eight-page Little Book.

Preview *The Big Game* by reading the title aloud to the class. Allow students time to look through the book and examine the pictures. Ask students to follow along and track the words in the Little Book as you read the story aloud to them.

Engage the class in the story. Draw upon students' experiences and feelings about the story to spark their interest. Ask them questions such as *What kind of sports do you like to play? What is it like to play or watch an exciting game? How does it feel to win? How does it feel to lose?*

Revisit the story. Lead the class in a second reading of *The Big Game*. This time, ask for volunteers to read aloud one page at a time. After each page is read, ask questions focusing on the content of the story. Here are some examples:

• *Why is this book called* The Big Game?
• *How do you think Bob feels when he misses his shot?*
• *What do the Phonics Team members do after they win?*
• *What do the Phonics Team members do with their pets after the game?*

INCLUDING ALL LEARNERS

More Phonics Team Stories
(Auditory/Visual Learners)

Materials: drawing paper, crayons or markers

Distribute the drawing materials, and ask students to come up with new stories with the Phonics Team members. Let students work with partners to write and illustrate a new adventure. Model how to make a Little Book, if they wish. When they are finished, they can read aloud their new stories and display their illustrations on a bulletin board. Invite volunteers to act out their new stories as well.

Make a Cheer!
(Auditory Learners)

Divide the class into pairs or small groups. Challenge the groups to come up with short sports cheers of their own. Allow them time to practice the cheers once they have written them. Offer them some cues for the cheers; for example, repeat three different action words three times each and then say the three different action words once each.

> Go, go, go!
> Run, run, run!
> Win, win, win!
> Go, run, win!

When they are ready, invite the groups to perform their cheers for the rest of the class.

Story Time
(Extra Help)

Give students extra time to read the story quietly. Invite students to give oral summaries of what happens in the story. Then encourage them to think about a time when they won an important game or sport. Invite students to share their stories with the rest of the class.

It's the last basketball game of the school year.

Boys and girls are jumping and shouting.

"Go for the hoop! Go for the hoop!"

Drums beat. Horns toot.

"T!...E!...A!...M!
T!...E!...A!...M!"

2

7

4

Bob runs down the floor and shoots.

Oops! He misses the hoop.

Kate gets the ball and throws it to Mike.

Mike runs around Bob and shoots from outside.

The ball bounces off the hoop.

Bev jumps, tips it in, and scores!

Drums beat. Horns toot.

5

Say It!

Give students time to read the story quietly. Then engage the class in a discussion about the words they read in the story. *What letter sounds do you know in the words? Which words have the /ü/ sound? The /ou/ sound? The /oi/ sound?*

Write It!

Challenge students to look through their Little Book *The Big Game* and list the words with dipthongs. Let them fold a piece of paper into four sections; label each *oo, ou, ow, oy;* and then list the words in the appropriate columns.

Family Connection

Send home the Little Book *The Big Game.* Encourage students to read the book to a family member.

BOOK CORNER

/ü/ oo
Puss in Boots
by Charles Perrault

/ou/ ou
The House That Jack Built
by David Cutts

/ou/ ow
Brown Bear, Brown Bear, What Do You See? by Bill Martin, Jr.

/ü/ oo, /oi/ oi
Too Much Noise
by Ann McGovern

/oi/ oy
Grandma's Joy
by Eloise Greenfield

Answer Key

UNIT 1   Short Vowels: a, o, i

page 2 – 2. a 3. e 4. b 5. d
page 3 – 2. cat 3. bag 4. van 5. hat
page 4 – 2. e 3. a 4. c 5. b
page 5 – 2. can 3. can 4. cannot 5. cannot
page 6 – 2. c 3. d 4. e 5. a
page 7 – 2. is 3. is 4. is not 5. is not
page 8 – 2. b 3. a 4. c; 2. off 3. on
page 11 – 2. yes 3. no 4. yes 5. no

UNIT 2   Short Vowels: u, e

page 12 – 2. d 3. a 4. e 5. c
page 13 – 2. rug 3. sun 4. nut 5. bug
page 14 – 2. d 3. e 4. a 5. b
page 15 – 2. no 3. no 4. yes 5. yes
page 16 – 3. bells 4. bags 5. a dog 6. cats 7. nuts
     8. bugs
page 19 – 2. Gus 3. Nan 4. red 5. rock 6. sits

UNIT 3   Blends

page 20 – 2. a 3. e 4. c 5. d
page 21 – 2. no 3. yes 4. no 5. no 6. no 7. no 8. no
     9. yes 10. yes
page 22 – 2. d 3. a 4. e 5. b
page 23 – 2. d 3. b 4. c 5. a
page 24 – 2. jump 3. milk 4. tank 5. gift
page 25 – 2. desk 3. tent 4. nest 5. Help
page 26 – 2. no 3. no 4. yes 5. no 6. no 7. yes 8. no
     9. no 10. yes
page 29 – 2. dog 3. hit 4. jump 5. bus 6. pens 7. grass
     8. desk 9. sits 10. dress

UNIT 4   Long Vowels: a

page 30 – 2. d 3. e 4. b 5. a
page 31 – 2. gray 3. plate 4. say 5. wakes
page 32 – 2. e 3. b 4. a 5. c
page 33 – 2. no 3. no; 2. socks 3. hats
page 34 – 2. d 3. c 4. a; 2. run 3. snack
page 37 – 2. no 3. no 4. no 5. no 6. no 7. yes 8. no
     9. yes 10. no

UNIT 5   Long Vowels: i

page 38 – 2. a 3. e 4. c 5. b
page 39 – 2. bike 3. I 4. fly 5. smile 6. cries
page 40 – 2. night 3. right 4. bright 5. high 6. light
page 41 – 2. no 3. yes 4. no 5. yes 6. no 7. no 8. yes
     9. no 10. yes
page 42 – 2. sand 3. wide 4. face 5. man 6. night 7. sky
     8. tire 9. nine 10. jog 11. hot 12. page
     13. run 14. train 15. yell 16. day 17. class
     18. snail
page 45 – Answers will vary.

UNIT 6   Long Vowels: o, e, u

page 46 – 2. d 3. a 4. e 5. b
page 47 – 2. snow 3. blow 4. window 5. grow
page 48 – 2. yes 3. no 4. yes 5. yes 6. no 7. yes
     8. no 9. yes 10. no

page 49 – 2. big 3. no 4. cold 5. cannot 6. is 7. on
     8. slow 9. rain 10. hold 11. day 12. sad
page 50 – 2. c 3. d 4. e 5. a
page 51 – 2. yes 3. no 4. yes 5. no 6. no 7. yes 8. yes
page 52 – 2. donkey 3. puppy 4. twenty 5. monkey
page 53 – 2. ears 3. clear 4. years 5. near
page 54 – 2. c 3. a 4. e 5. b
page 55 – Answers will vary.
page 56 – 2. happy 3. low 4. sunny 5. above 6. hold
     7. feet 8. behind 9. day 10. huge 11. wait
     12. sleep 13. ride 14. get on
page 59 – 2. blow 3. grow 4. sport 5. tree 6. donkey
     7. music 8. blue

UNIT 7   Digraphs: sh, ph, th

page 60 – 2. e 3. b 4. c 5. a
page 61 – Mike: new bat; Pete: have a mitt;
     Mike: on the team; Pete: she can play;
     Mike: the big field
page 62 – 2. no 3. yes 4. yes 5. no 6. no
page 63 – 2. Bev 3. Bob 4. Pete 5. Rose 6. Sue
page 64 – 2. crash 3. hat 4. bone 5. make 6. jump
     7. boat 8. grow 9. math 10. sleep 11. line
     12. tree
page 67 – 2. those blue shoes 3. that yellow rain hat
     4. those green shoes 5. that red and blue cap
     6. that black hat 7. those red shoes

UNIT 8   Digraphs: wh, ng, ch, tch, wr, kn

page 68 – 2. g 3. a 4. f 5. c 6. d 7. e
page 69 – Answers will vary.
page 70 – 2. string 3. swing 4. king 5. swing 6. long
page 71 – 2. c 3. d 4. e 5. b 6. f 7. a 8. g
page 72 – 2. lunchbox 3. peach 4. chalk 5. chicken
page 73 – 2. watch 3. scratch 4. match 5. watch
page 74 – 2. wrong 3. wrong 4. right 5. wrong 6. wrong
     7. wrong 8. right 9. right 10. right 11. wrong
     12. right
page 77 – 2. when 3. that 4. shake 5. king 6. wrong
     7. shine 8. bath 9. wheat 10. write 11. shoe
     12. sheep 13. knee 14. know 15. whale
     16. scratch

UNIT 9   r-Controlled Vowels: ar, er, ir, ur

page 78 – 2. d 3. e 4. b 5. a
page 79 – 2. brother 3. winter 4. sister 5. father
page 80 – 2. yes 3. yes 4. no 5. yes 6. yes 7. no 8. yes
page 83 – 2. under 3. under 4. after 5. after 6. before

UNIT 10   Diphthongs: oo, ou, ow, oy, oi

page 84 – 2. e 3. a 4. b 5. d
page 85 – 2. loud 3. outside 4. bounce 5. around
page 86 – 2. crown 3. town 4. clown 5. down
page 87 – 2. yes 3. no 4. no 5. no 6. yes 7. no 8. yes
page 88 – 2. dog 3. duck 4. cat 5. pig 6. owl 7. sheep
     8. frog

Practice and Assessment

Practice and Assessment Pages

The following reproducible pages give further opportunities for practice and written assessment of students' unit-by-unit progress. There is one practice page and one assessment page for each unit and an answer key for all the pages.

Answer Key for Practice and Assessment Pages

UNIT 1
Short Vowels: a, o, i

Practice (page 94)
2. Drawing of a dog
3. Drawing of a mitt
4. Drawing of a hat

Assessment (page 95)
2. cat
3. man
4. mitt
5. dog
6. box
7. van
8. doll

UNIT 2
Short Vowels: u, e

Practice (page 96)
2. tub: no
3. map: yes
4. bug: yes
5. men: yes
6. box: yes
7. nut: yes
8. pen: yes
9. mitt: yes
10. rug: no
11. sun: no
12. hat: yes

Assessment (page 97)
2. sun
3. bus
4. tub
5. pen
6. leg
7. rug

UNIT 3
Blends

Practice (page 98)

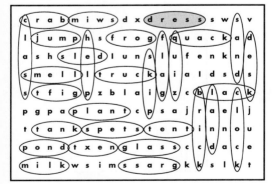

Assessment (page 99)
2. The plant is on the desk.
3. Tim has a gift.
4. The crab is on the sand.
5. Bob is next to the sled.
6. It is ten o'clock.
7. Bev can skip.

UNIT 4
Long Vowels: a

Practice (page 100)
2. pail
3. snail
4. snake
5. cage
6. crayon
7. cake

Assessment (page 101)
2. wakes
3. takes
4. waits
5. rain
6. plays
7. great
8. face

UNIT 5
Long Vowels: i

Practice (page 102)
Answers will vary.

Assessment (page 103)
2. cry, sky
3. fire, tire
4. light, night
5. hide, slide
6. mice, ice
7. nine, line
8. by, my
9. ride, side
10. eye, pie
11. high, my
12. sign, line

UNIT 6
Long Vowels: o, e, u

Practice (page 104)
Has Feet: Sue, goat, monkey, puppy, Pete, frog, donkey, dog
Has No Feet: window, rope, corn, soap, snow, snake, door, juice

Assessment (page 105)
Rose: snow, goat, bone, cold, go, soap, nose

hop: frog, jog, hot, pot, rock
Pete: eat, field, he, see, tree, sleep
pet: red, leg, men, ten, pen, sled

UNIT 7
Digraphs: sh, ph, th

Practice (page 106)
2. eight minus six equals two
3. ten minus seven equals three
4. five times three equals fifteen
6 and 7. Answers will vary.

Assessment (page 107)
2. A fish is on the dish.
3. Mike has earphones.
4. The baby takes a bath.
5. Gus races with Bob.

UNIT 8
Digraphs: wh, ng, ch, tch, wr, kn

Practice (page 108)
Answers will vary.

Assessment (page 109)
2. whistle
3. string
4. singing
5. cheese
6. watch
7. write
8. knife

UNIT 9
r-Controlled Vowels: ar, er, ir, ur

Practice (page 110)
Answers will vary.

Assessment (page 111)
Answers will vary.

UNIT 10
Diphthongs: oo, ou, ow, oy, oi

Practice (page 112)
Answers will vary.

Assessment (page 113)
2. food
3. shouts
4. sound
5. around
6. down
7. noise
8. boys

UNIT 1

Short Vowels: a, o, i

PRACTICE

Draw in the picture to match each sentence.

1. Nan has a <u>cat</u>.

2. Bob has a <u>dog</u>.

3. Tim has a <u>mitt</u>.

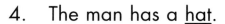

4. The man has a <u>hat</u>.

ASSESSMENT

Circle the word that matches the picture.

1.  hot hat hit

2. bat mat cat

3. map man mat

4. mat hill mitt

5. dog doll pot

6. six fox box

7. man pan van

8. doll hill ball

PRACTICE

Can it be on a bus?

A. Circle *yes* if you think it could be on a bus. Circle *no* if it could not.

1. leg   (yes)   no   7. nut   yes   no

2. tub   yes   no   8. pen   yes   no

3. map   yes   no   9. mitt   yes   no

4. bug   yes   no   10. rug   yes   no

5. men   yes   no   11. sun   yes   no

6. box   yes   no   12. hat   yes   no

B. If you circled *yes* beside a word, write the word on a line in the bus picture below.

leg

ASSESSMENT

bed	bell	bus	leg	pen	nut
rug	tub	bug	men	sun	ten

Write the word from the box that matches each picture.

1. _____ bed _____

2. _____

3. _____

4. _____

5. _____

6. _____

7. _____

Blends

PRACTICE

Is it in the box?

black	~~dress~~	help	pond	smell
brick	flag	jump	quack	steps
class	frog	land	quiz	swim
clock	gift	milk	sand	tank
crab	glass	next	skip	tent
desk	grass	plant	sled	truck

Circle each word from the list above when you find it in the puzzle.
Words can go forward, backward, or down.

```
c  r  a  b  m  i  w  s  d  x (d  r  e  s  s) s  w  s  v
l  j  u  m  p  h  s  f  r  o  g  f  q  u  a  c  k  a  d
a  s  h  s  l  e  d  l  u  n  s  l  u  f  e  n  k  n  e
s  m  e  l  l  l  t  r  u  c  k  a  i  a  l  d  s  d  s
s  t  f  i  g  p  z  b  l  a  i  g  z  c  b  l  a  c  k
p  g  p  a  p  l  a  n  t  c  p  s  a  j  r  a  e  l  j
t  t  a  n  k  s  p  e  t  s  t  e  n  t  i  n  n  o  u
p  o  n  d  t  x  e  n  g  l  a  s  s  c  c  d  a  c  e
m  i  l  k  w  s  i  m  s  s  a  r  g  k  k  s  l  k  t
```

ASSESSMENT

Make an *X* by the sentence that matches each picture.

1.    _____ The frog is in the box.
       __*X*__ The frog is in the grass.

2.   _____ The plant is on the desk.
       _____ The plant is on the dress.

3.    _____ Tim has a brick.
       _____ Tim has a gift.

4.    _____ The crab is on the steps.
       _____ The crab is on the sand.

5.    _____ Gus is next to the sled.
       _____ Bob is next to the sled.

6.   _____ It is ten o'clock.
       _____ It is six o'clock.

7.    _____ Bev can skip.
       _____ Bev can swim.

PRACTICE

Complete the crossword puzzle. Write the word for each picture.

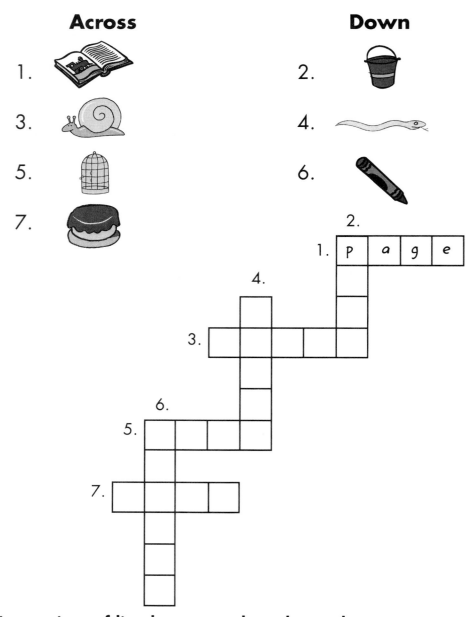

Across

1.

3.

5.

7.

Down

2.

4.

6.

Bonus: Using a piece of lined paper and a ruler, make your own crossword puzzle with long *a* words that you know.

ASSESSMENT

wakes	takes	waits	great
plays	~~say~~	rain	face

Write the word from the box that completes each sentence.

1. Bob and Nan _____*say*_____ , "Hey, Kate!"

2. Kate _____ up at 6:00.

3. Kate _____ a red pen off the desk.

4. Kate _____ at the bus stop.

5. Gus runs in the _____ and gets wet.

6. Kate _____ baseball.

7. The sun is up, and it's a _____ day.

8. Kate has a happy _____ .

PRACTICE

I like to ride...

a bike	on a train	~~on a plane~~	on skates	on a bug
on a bus	in a van	on a fox	in a truck	

Write a list of the things you like to ride. You can use the words in the box above.

on a plane

_____   _____

_____   _____

_____   _____

_____   _____

I like to...

play baseball	play basketball	play tennis	~~play games~~	run
play dolls	fly a kite	slide on a slide	swim	help

Write a list of the things you like to do. You can use the words in the box above.

play games

_____   _____

_____   _____

_____   _____

_____   _____

Long Vowels: i

ASSESSMENT

Rhymes

Say each word. Circle the two words that rhyme.
Write the two rhyming words on the line.

1. line (bike) lake (like)   bike   like
    _____

2. cry ride ice sky   _____

3. kite fire tire five   _____

4. light nine wide night   _____

5. hide smile high slide   _____

6. face mice ice my   _____

7. nine line night smile   _____

8. mice Mike by my   _____

9. ride right side kite   _____

10. bike eye bite pie   _____

11. five high my fire   _____

12. sign line side sky   _____

PRACTICE

Feet or No Feet?

~~boat~~	goat	corn	~~deer~~	door	donkey
window	monkey	soap	puppy	Pete	juice
Sue	rope	snow	snake	frog	dog

Read the words in the box above. List the things with feet under "Has Feet."
List the things without feet under "Has No Feet."

Has Feet	**Has No Feet**
deer	boat

ASSESSMENT

Rose / Hop

~~rope~~	~~dog~~	goat	jog	hot	soap	pot
snow	frog	bone	cold	go	nose	rock

Say each word in the box above.
If the word has a long **o** sound, as in *Rose*, write it on the line after "Rose."
If it has a short *o* sound, as in *hop*, write it on the line after "hop."

o like R**o**se _rope_ _____

_____

o like h**o**p _dog_ _____

_____

Pete / Pet

~~feet~~	~~bed~~	he	leg	men	tree	pen
eat	field	red	see	ten	sleep	sled

Say each word in the box above.
If the word has a long *e* sound, as in *Pete*, write it on the line after "Pete."
If it has a short *e* sound, as in *pet*, write it on the line after "pet."

e like P**e**te _feet_ _____

_____

e like p**e**t _bed_ _____

_____

UNIT 7

Digraphs: sh, ph, th

Math Problems in English

$7 + 5 = ?$

+	**plus**
−	**minus**
×	**times**
÷	**divided by**
=	**equals**

1	one	9	nine	17	seventeen
2	two	10	ten	18	eighteen
3	three	11	eleven	19	nineteen
4	four	12	twelve	20	twenty
5	five	13	thirteen	21	twenty-one
6	six	14	fourteen	22	twenty-two
7	seven	15	fifteen	23	twenty-three
8	eight	16	sixteen	24	twenty-four

A. Write the words for these math problems. Write your own answers
for numbers 3 and 4.

1. $2 + 4 = 6$ _two plus four equals six_

2. $8 - 6 = 2$ _____

3. $10 - 7 = ?$ _____

4. $5 \times 3 = ?$ _____

B. Using the numbers above, make up your own math problems.
Write the numbers and the English words.

1. ____ $3 + 9 = 12$ ____ _three plus nine equals twelve_

2. _____

3. _____

ASSESSMENT

Make an _X_ by the sentence that matches each picture.

1.

   _____ A sheep is by the boat.

   ___X___ A ship is by the boat.

   _____ A shoe is by the boat.

2.

   _____ A fish is on the dish.

   _____ A fish is on the dress.

   _____ A fish is on the desk.

3.

   _____ Mike has elephants.

   _____ Mike has telephones.

   _____ Mike has earphones.

4.

   _____ The baby takes a bat.

   _____ The baby takes a bath.

   _____ The baby takes a bus.

5.

   _____ Gus swims with Bob.

   _____ Gus splashes with Bob.

   _____ Gus races with Bob.

PRACTICE

What is it?

Finish each question with your own idea. Write the words on the line.
Ask a friend to guess the answer.

1. What is _____ *huge and gray and has four feet?* _____

    Answer: _____ *elephant* _____

2. What swims and _____?

    Answer: _____

3. What eats _____ and has _____?

    Answer: _____

4. What likes _____ and _____?

    Answer: _____

5. What is thin and _____ and _____?

    Answer: _____

6. What can jump and _____?

    Answer: _____

UNIT 8

Digraphs: wh, ng, ch, tch, wr, kn

Write the word that completes each sentence.

1. A _____*whale*_____ is a big sea animal like a fish.
   wheel / whale

2. A _____ is what an umpire blows to stop a game.
   whistle / wheel

3. A kite has a long _____ .
   swing / string

4. Sue is happy when she is _____ a song.
   singing / washing

5. Pete has a _____ sandwich in his lunchbox.
   beach / cheese

6. Bob has a _____ that says three o'clock.
   watch / match

7. You can _____ with a pen.
   right / write

8. You can eat meat with a _____ and fork.
   knee / knife

PRACTICE

My Family Members

Write the name(s) of your family member(s) on the lines.
Write *none* if you don't have that family member.

Family Member	**Name(s)**

1. Mother (or stepmother) _____

2. Sister(s) _____

    _____

    _____

3. Father (or stepfather) _____

4. Brother(s)_____

    _____

    _____

5. Grandmother(s) and Grandfather(s) _____

    _____

    _____

6. Others in my family _____

    _____

ASSESSMENT

Months and Weather

January	April	July	October
February	May	August	November
March	June	September	December

Say the months with your teacher. Then read the phrases below.

~~birds making nests~~	snow on the trees	gardens with big corn
ice on the car windows	new baby farm animals	yellow leaves blowing
hot days at the beach	sunburn on your arms	dark sky and clear stars

What months can have this weather? Write the phrases that match the months where you live.

1. March, April, May _____birds making nests_____

   _____

2. December, January, February _____

   _____

3. June, July, August _____

   _____

4. September, October, November _____

   _____

UNIT 10
**Diphthongs: oo, ou
ow, oy, oi**

PRACTICE

The Rooms of My House

Draw a floor plan or diagram of your own house or apartment. Label the rooms.

```
| Bedroom    |   Door →   | Kitchen     |
|------------|------------|-------------|
| Dining room | Family room            |
```

Write about your house or apartment.

_____

_____

ASSESSMENT

My House

Write the word that completes each sentence.

1. Oops! My brown _____ *boots* _____ are in the classroom.
    boots / boats

2. Oops! My lunchbox has old _____ in it.
    roof / food

3. The team _____ when the ball goes in the hoop.
    shouts / crown

4. Sue hears the loud _____ of thunder outside.
    town / sound

5. The classroom clock has numbers _____ it.
    around / under

6. Nan's bag is _____ on the floor by her desk.
    clown / down

7. The voices in the class make _____ .
    noise / rose

8. The sign on the door of the toilet says "_____" on it.
    Cows / Boys

Songs

	Unit 1 Short Vowels: a, o, i		Unit 4 Long Vowels: a
Short a	If You're <u>Happy</u>	Long a	<u>Rain Rain</u> Go <u>Away</u>
	The <u>Ants</u> Go Marching One by One		Down by the <u>Bay</u>
	<u>Sally</u> the <u>Camel Has</u> One Hump		I've Been Working on the <u>Railroad</u>
	<u>Happy</u> Birthday to You		When the <u>Saints</u> Go Marching In
Short o	<u>Donkey</u> Riding	Soft c / g	London <u>Bridge</u>
	On <u>Top</u> of Old Smoky		Three Blind <u>Mice</u>
Short i	<u>Itsy Bitsy</u> Spider		**Unit 5 Long Vowels: i**
	<u>Little</u> White Duck	Long- i	This Little <u>Light</u> of <u>Mine</u>
	<u>Little</u> Tom <u>Tinker</u>		There Was an Old Lady Who Swallowed a <u>Fly</u>
	Unit 2 Short Vowels: u, e		All <u>Night,</u> All Day
Short u	<u>Sun, Sun,</u> Mr. Golden <u>Sun</u>		<u>I'm</u> a Little Teapot
	The Wheels on the <u>Bus</u>		B-<u>I</u>-N-G-O
	<u>Hush,</u> Little Baby		**Unit 6 Long Vowels: o, e, u**
	You Are My <u>Sunshine</u>	Long o	<u>Row, Row, Row</u> Your Boat
Short e	<u>Head</u>, Shoulders, Knees, and Toes		Michael <u>Row</u> the <u>Boat</u> Ashore
	<u>Clementine</u>		<u>Open,</u> Shut Them (hands song)
	<u>Red</u> River Valley		<u>Hokey Pokey</u>
	<u>Lemon</u> Tree		This <u>Old</u> Man
	Unit 3 Blends		Dry <u>Bones</u>
	<u>Blue</u> Bird		<u>Home</u> on the Range
	Golden <u>Slippers</u>	Long e	Do Your <u>Ears</u> Hang Low?
	The <u>Green Grass Grows</u> All Around		I Like to <u>Eat, Eat, Eat, Eeples</u> and <u>Baneenees</u>
	I'm a Little <u>Green Frog</u>		There's a Little <u>Wheel</u> a Turnin'
	<u>Swing</u> Low <u>Sweet</u> Chariot		Are You <u>Sleeping?</u>
	Three Little Ducks…<u>Quack, Quack, Quack</u>	Long u	Skip to My <u>Lou</u>
			Oh, <u>Susanna</u>
			<u>Kumbaya</u>

Unit 7 Digraphs: sh, ph, th

<u>She'll</u> Be Coming Round the Mountain

Mrs. <u>Murphy's</u> Chowder

<u>This</u> Land Is Your Land

<u>There's</u> a Hole in the Bottom of the Sea

<u>Where</u> Is <u>Thumbkin?</u>

Unit 8 Digraphs: wh, ng, ch, tch, wr, kn

Oh <u>Where</u>, Oh <u>Where</u> Has My Little Dog Gone?

He's Got the <u>Whole</u> World

<u>Rachel, Rachel</u>, I've Been <u>Thinking</u>

Good <u>Morning</u>

<u>Ting</u>-a Lay-o

<u>Jingle</u> Bells

Do You <u>Know</u> the Muffin Man?

Unit 9 r-Controlled Vowels: ar, er, ir

The <u>Farmer</u> in the Dell

The <u>Bear</u> Went <u>over</u> the Mountain

Put <u>Your Finger</u> in the <u>Air</u>

Old MacDonald Had a <u>Farm</u>

Down by the <u>Station</u>

If I Had a <u>Hammer</u>

Unit 10 Diphthongs: oo, ou, ow, oy

<u>Looby Loo</u>

<u>Kookaburra</u>

Going to the <u>Zoo</u>

Take Me <u>out</u> to the Ball Game

<u>Down</u> by the Station

Danny <u>Boy</u>

Billy <u>Boy</u>

ESL Standards

National TESOL ESL Goals and Standards for Pre-K–12 Students

The following is excerpted with permission from *ESL Standards for Pre-K-12 Students* published by Teachers of English to Speakers of Other Languages, Inc. copyright 1997.

(TESOL refers to teachers of English to speakers of other languages. ESL refers to English as a second language. ESOL refers to English to speakers of other languages.)

GOALS FOR ESOL LEARNERS

TESOL has established three broad goals for ESOL learners at all age levels–goals that include personal, social and academic uses of English. Each goal is associated with three distinct standards. In TESOL's vision, ESOL learners will meet these standards as a result of the instruction they receive, thereby achieving the goals. Our schools need to ensure that all students achieve the English language competence needed for academic success and for life in a literate culture.

Goal 1:
To use English to communicate in social settings

A primary goal of ESL instruction is to assist students in communicating effectively in English, both in and out of school. Such communication is vital if ESOL learners are to avoid the negative social and economic consequences of low proficiency in English and are to participate as informed participants in our democracy. ESOL learners also need to see that there are personal rewards to be gained from communicating effectively in English. This goal does not suggest, however, that students should lose their native language proficiency.

Standards for Goal 1

Students will:

1. use English to participate in social interaction

2. interact in, through, and with spoken and written English for personal expression and enjoyment

3. use learning strategies to extend their communicative competence

Goal 2:
To use English to achieve academically in all content areas

In school settings, English competence is critical for success and expectations for ESOL learners are high. They are expected to learn academic content through the English language and to compete academically with native-English-speaking peers. This process requires that learners use spoken and written English in their schoolwork.

Standards for Goal 2

Students will:

1. use English to interact in the classroom

2. use English to obtain, process, construct, and provide subject matter information in spoken and written form

3. use appropriate learning strategies to construct and apply academic knowledge

Goal 3:
To use English in socially and culturally appropriate ways

ESOL students in U.S. schools come into contact with peers and adults who are different from them, linguistically and culturally. The diversity in U.S. schools mirrors the diversity in this country and around the world that young people will encounter as they move into the twenty-first century world of work. In order to work and live amid diversity, students need to be able to understand and appreciate people who are different and communicate effectively with them. Such communication includes the ability to interact in multiple social settings.

Standards for Goal 3

Students will:

1. use the appropriate language variety, register, and genre according to audience, purpose, and setting

2. use nonverbal communication appropriate to audience, purpose, and setting

3. use appropriate learning strategies to extend their sociolinguistic and sociocultural competence

Word List

a	bike	cold	fence	groups	it
above	birds	come/s	few	grow	it's
after	bite	corn	field	Gus	jack-in-the-box
age	black	cow	fifteen	gym	jog
all	blow	crab	fill	hail	juice
am	blue	crash/es	fire	hand	jump/s
an	boat	crayon	fish	hang/s	just
and	Bob	crown	five	happy	Kate
animals	bones	cry/cries	flag	has	king
apple	boots	cube	flat	hat	kitchen
are	bounce/s	dark	float/s	have	kite
arm	box	dash/es	floor	he	knee
around	boy	day	flute	head	knife
ask	brick	deer	fly	hear/s	know
at	bright	desk	food	help/s	lake
away	brother	dining room	for	her	lamp
ax	brown	dishes	forks	hey	land/s
baby	brush	do	four	hi	last
back	bug	dog	fourteen	hide	lay/s
bag	bus	doll	fox	high	leaf
ball	but	donkey	frog	hill	leaves
balloons	by	don't	from	him	left
bananas	bye	door	front	his	leg
barn	cage	down	fruit	hit/s	let
baseball	cake	dress	fun	hold/s	let's
basketball	can	drink	game	home	life
bat	cannot	drop	garden	home plate	lights
bath	can't	drum	get/s	hoop	like/s
bathroom	cap	duck	gift	hop/s	line
bathtub	car	earphones	girl	horn	little
beach	cat	ears	glad	hot	lives
beat	catch	eats	glass	hot dogs	living room
bed	chalk	eight	glide	house	long
bedroom	cheese	elephant	glue	how	lot
before	chicken	eleven	go	hug/s	loud
behind	class	eyes	goat	huge	low
bell	clear	face	gone	hurt/s	lunch
below	clock	falls	grapes	I	lunchbox
belt	closet	farm	graph	ice	mad
beside	clothes	fast	grass	in	make/s
between	clouds	fat	gray	inside	man
Bev	clown	father	great	is	many
big	coat	feet	green	isn't	(continued on next page)

117

map	on	rhyme	sleep/s	ten	under
mat	one	riddle	slide	tennis	up
match	onto	ride/s	slip	tent	us
math	oops	right	slow	test	uses
meat	open	ring	smell	that	van
men	opposites	road	smile	the	voices
mice	outside	rock	snack	then	wait/s
Mike	over	roof	snail	these	wake/s
miles	owl	rope	snake	thick	walk/s
milk	page	Rose	snow	thin	want
minutes	pail	rowboat	soap	things	wash/es
miss/es	pan	rug	socks	think	watch
mitt	pants	run/s	sofa	this	watch/es
mix	park	sad	song	those	water
monkey	peach	same	sound	three	wave/s
months	pedals	sand	soup	throw	weather
more	pen	sandwich	spill/s	thumb	well
mother	pet	say/s	splash/es	thump	wet
mouth	Pete	school	sports	thunder	whale
music	phone	score	stage	till	what
my	phonics	scoreboard	stars	Tim	wheat
name	Phonics Team	scratch	stay	time	wheel
Nan	photo	sees	steps	tip	when
near	picnic	seven	stick	tire	which
nest	pie	shake/s	stop	to	whistle
new	pig	she	string	today	white
next	pitch	sheep	students	toilet	wide
nice	plant	shelf	Sue	too	win
night	plate	shine	summer	toot	wind
nine	play/s	ship	sun	top	window
no	plop	shirt	sunburn	town	winter
noise	pond	shoes	sunny	toys	with
nose	pop/s	shorts	sunshine	train	write
not	pot	shout/s	swim/s	tree	wrong
nothing	problem	shoots	swing	truck	years
now	puppy	side	Tab	T-shirt	yell/s
numbers	purple	sign	table	tub	yellow
nurse	quack	sing/s	take/s	tune	yes
nut	quiz	sister	tan	turtles	you
o'clock	race/s	sit/s	tank	TV	your
of	rain	six	tap/s	twelve	yourself
off	raincoat	skip/s	team	twenty	
oh	reads	sky	telephone	two	
old	red	sled	tell	umpire	

Pronunciation Key

Pronunciation Key: Letter—Sound Relationships

Vowel Sounds

/a/   N**a**n, T**a**b, c**a**t

/ā/   K**a**te, r**ai**n, pl**ay**, gr**ea**t

/ä/   f**a**ther, w**a**lk

/är/   c**ar**, f**ar**m

/ār/   ch**air**

/e/   B**e**v, h**ea**d

/ē/   P**e**te, s**ee**, m**e**, r**ea**d, monk**ey**, bab**y**, n**ea**r, h**e**re, d**ee**r

/èr/   h**er**, g**ir**l, n**ur**se

/i/   T**i**m, s**i**t

/ī/   M**i**ke, p**ie**, m**y**, n**igh**t, H**i**, f**i**re, **i**ce

/o/   B**o**b, d**o**g,

/ō/   R**o**se, **o**ld, b**oa**t, n**o**, sl**ow**, c**o**rn, d**oo**r, sc**o**reb**oa**rd, f**ou**r

/ô/   s**o**ng, dr**aw**

/oi/   n**oi**se, t**oy**s

/ou/   c**ow**, l**ou**d,

/u/   G**u**s, s**u**n

/ù/   b**oo**k, p**u**t

/ü/   S**u**e, fl**u**te, f**oo**d, s**ou**p, j**ui**ce

/ū/   m**u**sic, f**ew**

/ə/   th**e**, **a**round, penc**i**l

Consonant Sounds

/b/   **b**ag

/d/   **d**og

/f/   **f**at, **ph**one, gi**f**t

/g/   **g**oat

/h/   **h**op

/j/   **j**og, ca**g**e

/k/   ro**ck**, **K**ate, **c**at, **c**lo**ck**

/ks/   so**cks**, bo**x**

/kw/   **qu**iz, **qu**ack

/l/   **l**amp, c**l**ass, p**l**ant, mi**l**k, hi**ll**

/m/   **m**at, ju**m**p, swi**mm**ing

/n/   **n**ot, sa**n**d, te**nn**is, **kn**ow

/p/   **p**ot, ha**pp**y

/r/   **r**un, g**r**ass, f**r**og, **wr**ite

/s/   **s**wim, fa**s**t, fa**c**e, dre**ss**

/t/   **t**ake, mi**tt**

/v/   **v**an

/w/   **w**ait

/y/   **y**es

/z/   **z**oo, jog**s**

/ch/   **ch**icken, bea**ch**, wa**tch**

/sh/   **sh**ip, fi**sh**

/th/   **th**in, wi**th**

/<u>th</u>/   **th**e, **th**is, **th**at

/hw/   **wh**at, **wh**en, **wh**ere

/ng/   si**ng**

The following irregular words are not pronounced the way they are spelled. Each irregular word is listed below with a respelling to help you pronounce it.

above (əbuv), *ball* (bôl), *bananas* (bənanəz), *bounce* (bouns), *cheese* (chēz), *clothes* (klōz), *comes* (kumz), *do* (dü), *doll* (dol), *don't* (dōnt), *door* (dōr), *eight* (āt), *eyes* (īz), *face* (fās), *four* (fōr), *gone* (gôn), *great* (grāt), *has* (haz), *have* (hav), *hey* (hā), *huge* (hūj), *ice* (īs), *is* (iz), *isn't* (izənt), *juice* (jüs), *little* (litəl), *lives* (livz), *many* (menē), *minutes* (minits), *of* (əv), *off* (ôf), *one (wun)*, *page* (pāj), *quiz* (kwiz), *rhymes* (rīmz), *riddle* (ridəl), *rock* (rok), *scoreboard* (skōrbōrd), *shoes* (shüz), *sign* (sīn), *socks* (soks), *the* (thə), *thumb* (thum), *to* (tü), *two* (tü), *walk* (wôk), *want* (wônt), *what* (hwut), *whistle* (hwisəl)

Index

Bibliography

Adams, M. J. *Beginning to Read: Thinking and Learning About Print.* Cambridge: Massachusetts Institute of Technology, 1990.

Blevins, W. *Phonics from A to Z: A Practical Guide.* New York: Scholastic, 1998.

Chall, J. and Popp, H., *Teaching and Assessing Phonics.* Cambridge, Massachusetts: Educators Publishing Service Inc., 1996.

Foorman, B. R., Francis, D. J., Fletcher, J. M., Schatschneider, C., and Mehta, P. (1998). The role of instruction in learning to read: Preventing reading failure in at-risk children. *Journal of Educational Psychology* 90 (1–15).

Honig, B. *Teaching Our Children to Read: The Role of Skills in a Comprehensive Reading Program.* Thousand Oaks, CA; Corwin Press, 1996.

Moats, L. C. (1998). Teaching Decoding. *American Educator* 22 (42-49) Washington, D.C.: The American Federation of Teachers, AFL-CIO.

Samuels, S. J. (1988). Decoding and Automaticity: Helping Poor Readers Become Automatic at Word Recognition. *The Reading Teacher* (April).

Snider, V. E. (1995). A Primer on Phonemic Awareness: What It Is, Why It's Important, and How to Teach It. *School Psychology Review* 24 (3)

Treiman, R., and Baron, J. (1981). Segmental Analysis Ability: Development and Relation to Reading Ability. *Reading Research: Advances in Theory and Practice* (3).

Wiley, K. *Alligator at the Airport: A Language Activities Dictionary.* New York: Addison Wesley Longman, Inc., 1994.

Yopp, H. K. (1995). Read-aloud books for developing phonemic awareness: An annotated bibliography. *The Reading Teacher* 48 (6).